THE STARTUP TEACHER PLAYBOOK

THE STARTUP TEACHER

PLAYBOOK

Turn Your Ideas Into Actions,
Personalize Professional Development,
and Create Innovative Learning Experiences
for You and Your Students

WRITTEN BY
Michelle Blanchet & Darcy Bakkegard
ILLUSTRATED BY
Christian Bartsch

The Startup Teacher Playbook
© 2021 by Times 10 Publications

These books are available at special discounts when purchased in quantity for premiums, promotions, fundraising, and educational use. For inquiries and details, contact us at 10Publications.com.

Published by Times 10
Highland Heights, OH
10Publications.com

Cover and Interior Design by Steven Plummer
Editing by Carrie White-Parrish
Copyediting by Jennifer Jas

Library of Congress Cataloging-in-Publication Data is available.

ISBN: 978-1-948212-21-2
First Printing: January, 2021

For teachers everywhere.

Table of Contents

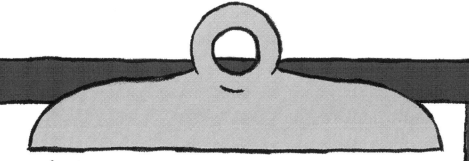

Module One:

An Introduction

to *The Startup Teacher Playbook* and An Invitation to Overhaul the System

In this Module:

- PD isn't working
- Our vision for what professional learning should be
- How *The Startup Teacher Playbook* feeds into our vision
- Rethinking how we "run" our classrooms
- Adapting what works: Startup methodology meets teacher PD
- Nurturing the desire to fix problems
- Make the case: Trust us to do our jobs
- What you'll get from this book
- Final thoughts

PD Isn't Working

And here you are again. It's a few days before school starts, but instead of preparing for your students and readying your classroom, where are you? Sitting listlessly in the auditorium through another one-size-fits-all, sit 'n' get professional development (PD) training for educators.

It's two hours in, and so far, nothing has been about your students, teaching, or your to-do list. You look around at the glazed eyes of your colleagues, still not fully comprehending why this torture must be endured multiple times throughout the year.

You stare up at the ceiling and do a bit of quick mental math:

- Speaker fee, flight, and lodging = a range from $1,000 to $10,000.

- Number of staff sitting (instead of doing), X training hours, X salaries = thousands of dollars.

- Number of times your students and their needs have been mentioned = few to none.

- Number of ideas generated to better support the students in your building = few.

- Amount of future time allotted for staff to use today's information to craft responses to student needs = little to none.

- Direct benefits to student learning, empowerment, productivity, or joy = too frustrating to calculate.

The numbers add up to a huge waste of time and money with little to no direct impact on student learning, empowerment, productivity, joy, purpose, or connection. Sure, the presenter said a few funny things and made a good general point or two, but still, you feel a knot tighten in your stomach and cannot quiet the voice in your head yelling, "I could be making progress on things that HELP students right now!"

You realize you have to make a choice. You may decide to:

1. **Laugh it off**. You're here and this is happening, so you might as well make the best of it. There's no point taking this presentation too seriously. You start to chat with your buddies, showing them pics from summer vacation, before drifting over to Facebook.

2. **Vent**. You know an end-of-the-day survey is coming—and if it doesn't, an email is happening—so you start crafting your response during the meeting. Perhaps if you are specific and explicit in your criticism, administration will make changes. You hope so, anyway. You've never been so excited to complete a feedback survey.

3. **Work**. It's not as efficient as being in your classroom, but you can sit in this meeting, (mostly) ignore the presenter, look down at your own materials, and prep as much as possible so maybe you can get home before dark.

> "Show me a room with 300 people and one keynote speaker, and I'll show you hundreds of people grading papers, writing lesson plans, or reading Facebook posts."
> – Mark Barnes, longtime educator

That's just the way it is, right? You have three basic choices: laugh it off, vent and hope, or ignore the presentation and do your own work. What you cannot choose, however, is how PD time, money, and energy are spent. All roads lead to the same narrow destination, and it turns out the choice in this adventure isn't yours. After all, you're not in charge of professional development or the decisions made at the district office. You can't control what's happening.

You're "just" a teacher.

What a crappy feeling. The utter powerlessness and futility; the waste of your time, expertise, and dedication. You know what your students need—you know what you need—but no one cares enough to ask you. Worse yet, it sometimes feels like no one respects you enough to ask.

We picked this story because it captures what we experienced as teachers in the US and abroad. After talking with teachers across the country, this scenario is shockingly universal: teachers of all grades, subjects, and experience levels are herded into a room, treated like they are all exactly the same and need the same training, and are generally taught the way they are told *not* to teach their students.

Meanwhile, students with actual needs and problems are heading their way, and all those teachers with all their experience and ideas are just sitting there, silent.

Schools offer professional learning with the best of intentions (we hope), but too often it feels like they gather bodies into a room to check off a box, rather than to look for ways to truly help educators grow professionally. Research by the New Teacher Project Report shows that overall, how schools go about professional development is incredibly ineffective:

- On average, districts spend $18,000 *per teacher* on professional learning.

- Teachers spend 10 percent of the school year in trainings.

- Yet there is no evidence that teaching and learning improve because of the PD schools provide.

Philosophical questions teachers ask themselves during irrelevant PD:

- Is there any data that shows higher standardized math test scores lead to improved quality of life at age twenty-five? Forty? Seventy?
- Does memorizing facts help you become a homeowner?
- Is getting straight A's a guaranteed path to happiness?
- Is there any data that all the data we're collecting is making any bit of difference on anything?

What if...
it wasn't like this?

What if professional development—and all those other meetings—was about students? About making teaching and learning better? About identifying challenges and problems in our classrooms and schools, and crafting solutions? What if we were trained to harness the collective wisdom and ingenuity of educators so we could transform education from the inside out?

We want you to know that all these "what ifs" *can* become the reality. This is your invitation to help us achieve that vision.

As we've traveled the country working with educators, it's been glaringly obvious that:

1. Teachers know what they're doing. They're the learning experts and have amazing ideas to improve education.

Yet...

2. Most training treats teachers like homogenous blobs, dishing out the same information and resources to all of them despite different needs, interests, strengths, and goals, not to mention the different needs of students.

Because...

3. Trainings and workshops tend to be structured, frequently grade/subject specific, or feature a generic speaker who shares cool ideas but doesn't help us build our own skills to implement them.

But...

4. If we had the right content and facilitation, training and PD *could* do so much more to nurture teachers' skills as leaders and support them with the time and tools to identify, develop, and implement their ideas to improve education.

Inspired by this untapped potential, we continued to develop our workshops to coach teachers to turn inspiration into reality. And it worked. Teachers left our workshops fired-up, armed with concrete action plans, and reported back on their success. We realized we were witnessing the slow drips of a revolution, as each teacher went back to their classroom or school to implement change. Inspired by them, we decided to open the floodgates and unleash the torrent of teacher potential.

Enter *The Startup Teacher Playbook*. Enter *you*.

Our Vision for What Professional Learning Should Be

We decided to write this book to give *you*—the teacher—a personal coach so you can organize and run PD relevant to *your* needs, challenges, and opportunities. We wanted to give you a cost-effective, time-efficient way to work on your own professional learning and simultaneously develop *your* ideas for your classroom and students. *The Startup Teacher Playbook* provides the structure and guidance you need to implement your great ideas. It provides an alternative to traditional PD; an alternative you can implement from the comfort of your classroom or home.

The premise for *The Startup Teacher Playbook* is simple:

> Skip the fads; stop bringing in all the consultants. Let's use PD as a space to give teachers time and credit for working on their own ideas and well-being so they can truly improve teaching and learning.

Simple, but somehow not that obvious.

Too often, professional learning is reactionary (give a man a fish), when we need professional learning that is visionary (teach a man to fish). Teacher training and PD must match teachers' needs and nurture their potential. It must assume that teachers are talented and capable, and allow them to pivot in the face of challenges. The PD content in this book goes beyond grade level and subject area to help you hone what's relevant for you and your students.

Our dream is to see more teachers in the educational driver's seat, leading from the classroom (or any other position). Imagine if, instead of spending 10 percent of our time in ineffective PD or meetings, we used that time to get proactive and address what *wasn't* working in our classrooms or schools, and then collaborate, ideate, and solve problems. Imagine if we used PD to nurture our skills and keep learning and evolving to stay ahead of the changing times. Or imagine if we spent that time on well-being, ensuring our mental health and preventing burnout.

It *could* be that way. After years of working with teachers, these are the three professional learning topics we feel most educators are missing out on and so desperately need to make that dream a reality:

1) Open-ended professional learning: Give teachers time to tinker, play, explore, and create.

We talk so much about hands-on, experiential learning for students, but then provide professional learning that is quite the opposite. Instead, we can promote PD time that lets teachers develop their own ideas, think through implementation, collaborate, and problem-solve. It's unnecessary to always have an agenda. Providing space for teachers to play and create will ultimately do more to support them as they develop and design their students' educational journeys.

Subjects like design thinking or changemaking do a lot to help teachers nurture the 4 C's (creativity, collaboration, critical thinking, and communication). Providing open-ended PD formats or unstructured time would give educators the opportunity to adapt learning as needed, enabling them to pivot in the face of an ever-changing educational landscape with evolving student needs and behaviors.

2) Leadership for teachers: Train all teachers to see themselves as leaders.

Education is a field based on relationships. Leadership is all about building relationships, so why aren't better leadership strategies in our PD repertoire? Teachers are leaders and can feel confident in their abilities and expertise in working with people. They can pursue ideas that would improve teaching and learning. By building these strengths in teachers, we can solve many of the challenges holding our students (and our schools) back. In addition, teachers can then seize the reins and organize and facilitate their own workshops, trainings, incubators, and accelerators as they share their expertise with each other.

3) Emotional intelligence for educators: Nurturing our social-emotional learning to prevent burnout.

We talk so much about social-emotional learning for students, but rarely take time to nurture our emotional intelligence prior to or during teaching. Teaching is a demanding job with a load of emotional baggage. When burnout strikes, we're left maintaining (at best), so innovating gets thrown out the window. Preventing burnout keeps us fresh and energized so we can continue to try new ideas and address challenges. Moreover, being metacognitive about self-care strategies to maintain our well-being will help us model these skills to our students.

How *The Startup Teacher Playbook* Feeds Into Our Vision

These basic principles are at the heart of our workshops and this book. *The Startup Teacher Playbook* will not spoon-feed you specific solutions to specific challenges. Instead, we walk the talk and provide you with concrete ways to find solutions for yourself, just like an entrepreneur would do. We discovered we could take what we had learned from the startup world and apply the same processes, methods, and models to the professional learning space.

The next modules in this playbook—Modules Two, Three, and Four—outline how you can use startup methodology and apply it to the education space to find big and small ways to lead your own learning experiences. Module Five includes professional learning resources, tools, and strategies to take your ideas to the next level.

In **Module Two,** you will define problems you want to solve and develop solutions. This is our way of giving you "open-ended time" to try out ideas, test them, and grow as an educator. Using the Educator Canvas—a tool similar to that used in startup methodology—you will have an opportunity to get proactive on challenges or to seize opportunities. You'll gain skills as you exercise your creativity and critical thinking, and find encouragement to take healthy risks for the benefit of your students.

> YES, you might be able to get actual credit for doing this work! See Module Five for an Impact Log.

In **Module Three,** you will reflect on your own leadership potential, and if you're meeting it. We know you have bold ideas to improve education for your students. How you interact and work with others will determine how far those ideas are able to go. Use the numerous activities and strategies in this module to expand your ideas and further strengthen the relationships you've built with students and colleagues (on whom your success will lie).

In **Module Four,** you will learn to take better care of yourself so you can innovate and meet the challenges of educating. Innovating can be hard. Just like in the startup world, if you don't take care of yourself, you can burn out. We offer you strategies and activities to help you nourish your well-being and build your mental stamina.

Finally, the resources in **Module Five** offer additional tools to help you as you go through this process. You will find templates and suggestions to help you collaborate, overcome obstacles, and generate new ideas to solve problems you're facing. Most importantly, we offer you a practical (and downloadable) Impact Log to help you get credit for learning about these topics, for innovating, and for developing yourself as an educator.

> Doing something new for PD does not mean lowering the standards. See how *The Startup Teacher Playbook* meets the Standards for Professional Learning on page 254.

In *The Startup Teacher Playbook*, we go beyond talking and give you ways to build skills and to *act*. These fundamental skills will enable you to adapt and react to the challenges you face daily so you're better equipped to give your students the high-quality education they deserve. Whether you're chomping at the bit to start implementing your 101 ideas for improving education, or you're still wrapping your head around the idea of taking action instead of waiting for solutions, we're here for you! Throughout *The Startup Teacher Playbook,* we provide guidance and support to help you find your voice, activate your ideas, and keep from letting "no" get in the way of you doing you.

Rethinking How We "Run" Our Classrooms

As you've already gathered, we're starting a grassroots revolution led by teachers to take back our PD, create the classrooms we crave and kids deserve, and generally do whatever we can from the educational trenches to make teaching and learning better for everyone involved. And we're counting on teachers like you to use the tools in this book—tools inspired by the startup world—to develop the skills necessary for this work. Even if you agree with all our talk about overhauling PD, you might be wondering: Why startup methodology? How did you two teachers make that leap?

We know it may sound abstract to talk about the startup world and how we can apply it to the education space. We get it. So before we can truly get into *The Startup Teacher Playbook*, we'd like to take a step back and take you through where this idea came from.

First, it must be said that we love learning lessons from other industries and applying them to our work as educators. For instance, we love how marketers strive to uncover ways to get people to *care* about an idea and to make an idea *sticky* enough for people to carry that idea with them. That's exactly what we try to do with our students every day: we spend countless hours figuring out ways to convince them that what we're teaching is important, and then we spend even more hours determining how to best present that knowledge so it *sticks* inside their brains. Needless to say, we've learned a lot from marketers.

When we found ourselves learning about the business world, it was only natural for us to explore the potential synergies with the education world. People have often told us that business and education don't go together, but we were curious enough to want to see if we could find an alignment. We weren't disappointed. Even with our "business for dummies" mentality, we were able to quickly spot lessons from which we could improve our work as educators.

Our first hook was what we learned about how to *run a* business and the clear fundamentals to successfully operate it. Our aha moment: why had we never been taught how to *run* a classroom? We realized no one had ever broken down the different processes we need to consider to create a fully functioning, operational classroom. It was assumed we would just know. Sure, we heard advice on planning lessons and managing discipline, resources for bulletin boards and flexible seating. But—we were never asked to look holistically at how we run our classrooms. No one had ever helped us consider that we could operationalize our classroom and manage it in different ways to create more efficient and productive systems.

For us, that was empowering. Businesses break down their processes into key fundamentals, which enables them to not only function better, but to better understand what's working and not working. It's like their business plan. We began to wonder if it would be easier to run successful classrooms if we were given a chance to define our processes and create a classroom "business plan" with more structure.

In case you aren't sure exactly what goes into a business plan, we'll save you a Google search. The fundamentals we focused on were People, Operations, Accounting, Strategy, Finance, and Marketing. While at first they might sound completely out of touch with the education space, they're surprisingly relevant: the questions they force someone to ask about their business are *very* similar to the questions we ask ourselves as educators.

Inspired to see how this might look in our classroom, we took these six basic business fundamentals (yes, we've oversimplified) and translated them to education. Our premise: if you better define your processes, you more clearly determine what's working and what needs to be improved.

Take a look at how these fundamentals play out in a sample business, and see how this compares to your approach to your classroom. Go ahead and answer these same questions as they relate to how you run your classroom.

The Lemonade Stand

Susan wants to open a lemonade stand so she can raise money for an upcoming field trip. She sits down to make a business plan, thinking through the basic fundamentals. Her goal: sell lemonade and secure the funds she needs to go on this field trip.

People: How will she motivate and engage her employees?

Susan asks her friend to join her venture and treats her as an equal. She knows her friend is excited to spend time with her and might need a bit of financial assistance so she can go on the field trip, too—two great motivating factors. Susan models how she expects her partner to act with and for customers, focusing on being kind and respectful while showing her friend the ropes. Susan knows they'll work well together.

Operations: How will she ensure everything runs smoothly? What needs to take place for her business to function?

Susan makes sure she and her friend have mastered their lemonade recipe. They borrow pitchers from family and neighbors to reduce costs. She makes sure to order supplies, keeps the stand clean, and checks that everyone understands their roles and responsibilities.

Accounting: How will she ensure they're profitable and achieving their goals?

She gets a cashbox, calculator, and notebook to track their expenses and income. They want to make $20 per day to achieve their field trip goal, so they calculate how much they will spend on each pitcher of lemonade and how much to charge for each cup.

Strategy: What tactics will she employ to ensure she meets goals and targets?

Susan and her friend check the forecast for the hottest days and ask their parents to help them set up a stand near a popular playground. They only operate during busy periods. They have two months to generate enough funds for the field trip. They decide that if they don't do well in the first two weeks, they will call it quits and try out another idea.

Finance: How will she manage assets and liabilities and plan for future growth?

Susan and her friend ask family members to donate the initial funds they will need to get started so they don't have to worry about debt or loans. They work together to decide how much of their earnings they should set aside for new supplies and/or to grow their business if they do really well.

Marketing: How will she draw people to her stand?

Visuals count. Susan and her friend have fun painting a beautiful banner full of color and pictures of lemons. They wear complementary dresses to give themselves a polished appearance.

Let's take these same fundamentals and apply them to how you run your classroom.

Your goal(s):

People:

How do you motivate and engage your students? How do you encourage them to tap into their strengths and reach their potential? How do you build relationships?

Operations:

What processes and tools do you need to make your classroom run smoothly?

Accounting:

How do you know students are mastering skills? How do you know they're enjoying school and learning how to work well with others?

Strategy:

What are your goals for the year? How will you achieve them? How do the projects and initiatives you have for the year scaffold toward your goals so you and your students can achieve them?

Finance:

How are you investing in yourself, your classroom, or your school for continuous growth and improvement?

Marketing:

How do you get buy-in from your students (e.g., in learning, in school in general)? How do you make core learning *sticky*?

How did it feel to operationalize your classroom? We hope these questions were useful and gave you insights into how you organize the different moving parts of your work. We hope it led you to articulate the different systems you put in place so you can identify and assess which areas are making teaching and learning successful, and which need work. You probably noticed that all of these areas can be—and sometimes *need* to be—altered at any time (mid-year, mid-day, mid-lesson!). Having a strategy to spot inefficiencies will make it easier to know where to invest your energy to make improvements.

Adapting What Works: Startup Methodology Meets Teacher PD

Even if you can see the value of breaking down your classroom into its fundamental parts, we understand if you're not crazy about the mere suggestion of comparing your classroom to a business. It may feel weird, almost sacrilegious, to talk about business in education. We get it. People picture greedy Wall Street types who define success by stock market value and cash assets. No, that's *not* teachers. But as mentioned in the subtitle, we are like **social entrepreneurs** (more on that in a bit).

> As defined by the World Economic Forum, social entrepreneurs use business principles to develop new approaches to solve old problems. They value impact over profit. Basically, it's using business to do good.

Businesses aim to create value through the goods and services they provide, often offering what people didn't even know they needed (how many times have you left Target with a few items you had no intention of purchasing?). That's what we do as teachers: create value for our students—and ultimately for society—by equipping them with the skills and knowledge they need to be successful.

In some ways, teachers act as social entrepreneurs. Our goal isn't profit, it's impact. Think about it: every year, you get a new batch of students, potentially a new course load, and new challenges. No matter who comes through the door, your job is to connect with them, discover their needs, and work with them to grow their skills so they can thrive in the world. This requires running an efficient classroom, one that's agile and can adapt to changing demands.

> Want to learn more about social entrepreneurship? Visit ashoka.org, the first and largest organization out there supporting social entrepreneurs.

For almost a decade, we've dabbled in the startup space—the social startup space—by starting our own venture and working with other social entrepreneurs as they develop theirs. The process has enabled us to gain a wealth of knowledge on how to get ideas off the ground, lead others, and allow processes and models to evolve with changing times so we can achieve our goals and make the impact we seek.

Social entrepreneurs grew out of the frustrating reality that policies and politics move slowly. Instead of sitting around and waiting, social entrepreneurs focus on what they can do now by asking, "How can we work within the system to solve problems and help others?"

Social entrepreneurs run social businesses.
Here's how they are different from "normal" businesses:

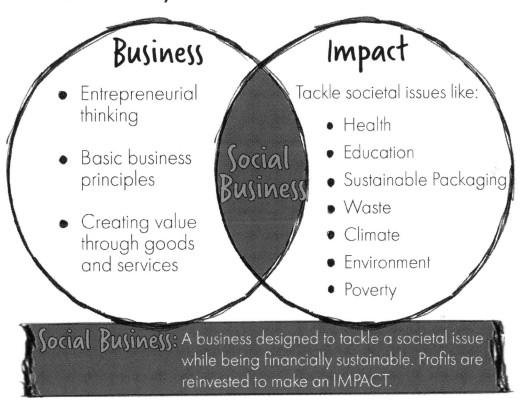

Business
- Entrepreneurial thinking
- Basic business principles
- Creating value through goods and services

Social Business

Impact
Tackle societal issues like:
- Health
- Education
- Sustainable Packaging
- Waste
- Climate
- Environment
- Poverty

Social Business: A business designed to tackle a societal issue while being financially sustainable. Profits are reinvested to make an IMPACT.

Educators face similar constraints. It's easy to say the system doesn't work (it frequently doesn't: policy isn't always in our favor, mandates are handed down from on high, and a lot of baggage comes with our job). But at the end of the day, we want what's best for our students. So how do we work within the system to make it better? How do we start with our own practice and with our own schools—no matter how small the steps may be—to make education as great as we know it can be?

Combining our experiences in the classroom with our experiences with social entrepreneurship, a clear answer emerged: Let's give teachers a chance to fix things. Let's give them the power to assess how we run our classrooms and schools, evaluate what's working or not working, and make the necessary changes so we can lead the types of educational experiences that will add the most value for our students. Adopting startup methodologies gave us a new way to explore how we might help educators evolve their role to meet modern demands and make radical changes in an industry that has remained relatively stagnant.

To get started, you just need an open mind and a little imagination, but a lot of what we're about to say is what you already do. It's just a new way to look at it.

We're asking you to think of your classroom as a startup.

You may be a brand new entrepreneur just launching this venture (*welcome, first year teachers*) or an established veteran (*thank you!*). Your classroom is your "storefront" and it's up to you to run your "company." It's a complicated venture, requiring all your blood, sweat, and (all too often) tears as you solve problems on every front. Your employees (students) look to you to lead, and your customers (parents/society) expect you to produce nothing short of magic. How are you going to make that happen?

In the lemonade activity, you were already defining how your classroom operates; consider that as the outline for how your startup (classroom) functions. Now let's take it a step further and get creative with how we define the roles we each serve (and our classroom serves) within this operation. In the same way that we can differentiate the moving parts of how our classroom works, we can also take a step back and differentiate between the contributions we make as teachers, those made by students, and the processes that frame the class(es) we teach. Take a look:

Think of your classroom* as your startup

Your classroom is an organic, evolving entity informed by the set of fundamental moving parts that you design. How you run your classroom can always change and adapt according to the needs of you, your students, and your circumstances (consider how shifting to online learning upended your "business plan"). Your classroom is that physical (or virtual) space that kids

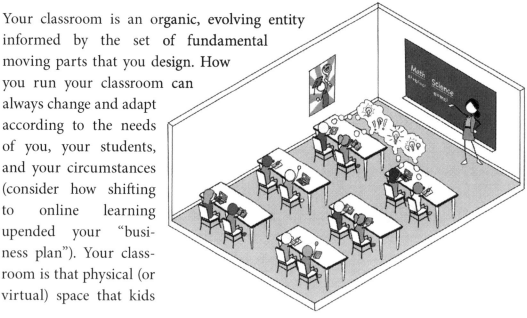

hopefully want to come to each day. It's where you and your students will spend countless hours each year, so make it a place everyone wants to be.

You = founder and CEO

You are in charge of designing the space and overseeing the processes and people that make it function. You will define the goals for your startup and work with your employees (your students) to craft a vision and mission and successfully work toward both. Establishing and materializing your vision and mission will deter-

*You are not your classroom. Treating it objectively will help you identify areas that are working and those that need improvement without feeling like it's a personal failure (because it's not).

mine how you create value and achieve impact. Be intentional with your goals. You set the tone, pace, energy, atmosphere, and, most importantly, the bar for what you and your students can accomplish. Don't just manage your classroom, lead it!

Your Employees = Your Students

Think of your students like employees, not customers or clients. You will work *with* them every day to generate success in your classroom. They will add value to the work you do, and ultimately their efforts will define the impact you create. Through ongoing evaluations, guidance, and mentoring, your leadership will enable them to meet their highest potential, and you to meet yours.

See? In the same way founders run startups by working with employees to provide goods or services to the world, we as educators work with our students to ensure they're equipped with the skills and knowledge they need to thrive in society. This requires us to view our classroom as an organic, evolving entity (similar to a startup) that we can shift and adapt to the changing demands of society and the needs of our students, so we can ultimately generate the greatest impact.

The best news: you don't necessarily need any specific or special training to get started. One striking feature about many social entrepreneurs is that they have no business background whatsoever. They are simply people from all walks of life who have ideas on how to address a challenge and want to learn how to apply business principles to do good. It's the will or desire to *do* something in the face of challenges that causes people to embrace these new ideas.

Many teachers have ideas about how to address educational challenges. As we built the foundation for this book, we realized we didn't need to do anything radical; we just needed to nurture a desire that was already there and help educators break down problems into manageable parts that they could fix.

Nurturing the Desire to Fix Problems

One big difference between people who enter the social startup scene and those who enter the education scene is *the level of support.* Teachers are not trained in solving challenges, nor provided a systematic approach to doing so. Yet solving challenges can lead to our greatest impact. Social entrepreneurs are supported and encouraged to take risks and tap into their values when the going gets tough. Teachers aren't.

Think back to the Choose Your Adventure at the beginning of this section. The lack of choice, the lack of control, limits the potential of educators and slows innovation. Training should support teachers to *solve challenges* and *adapt* to the dynamic needs of students. We need safe outlets where we can take healthy risks for the sake of our students, a place to ask ourselves the questions to design learning experiences that best cater to the needs, strengths, and interests of students.

This is where our talk about professional learning and the startup world over-laps. We want to give you the space and the support so you can test your ideas. This playbook is just that: a system to develop your great ideas and get them off the ground. Being a Startup Teacher has nothing to do with creating an actual startup; it's about cultivating the mentality to see a problem and try to fix it.

> **Can you imagine professional learning opportunities where you devote time toward your ideas and receive support to develop them? This takes place in the business world. Imagine if we replicated accelerators and incubators in the education space. What could we accomplish?**

	Accelerators	Incubators
Business World	Programs designed to further develop or "accelerate" the existing ideas or models. They tend to offer intensive support over a limited period of time.	Programs or spaces to help develop or "incubate" new ideas. They are a lot less structured but offer a space and support to get ideas off the ground.
Education Space	Imagine fellowship opportunities within your district to get funding and mentorship to develop the great ideas you're working on in your classroom and school.	Imagine spaces in your building or community where educators could go to freely develop their ideas to improve teaching and learning. This provides a chance to play with and pilot new ideas in a safe space.

PD is the ideal space to *fix* the problems that prevent us from doing our jobs to the best of our abilities. In a world that's changing fast, we need to be able to adapt teaching and learning faster than the system allows. PD offers the ideal outlet for us to embrace this work. From our experience as trainers, we know teachers are thirsty to do *more*, to improve teaching and learning, and to improve education in general. We have the time in education to do this work; we just need to tap into the time we're not using effectively and do something new with it.

That's why you're here.
That's what this book is for.
After all, if not now, when? If not you, who?

A Startup Story by Michelle

As a social studies teacher, I didn't realize that I would someday enter the business space. It wasn't until I went abroad for my master's degree that I learned about social impact and discovered the world of social business. It was inspiring, especially the concept of the social entrepreneur who uses business principles to solve societal problems.

What was so enticing about this space was that so many of the people in it had absolutely no experience in business. They were people who had ideas on how to solve problems and wanted to help. What was even more inspiring was how quickly the movement spread. Around the globe, people and organizations began to set up workshops and incubators to help individuals get their ideas off the ground–to help ordinary citizens gain the skillset and mindset to create positive change for their communities. From Madrid to Zurich to Geneva and back to the US, I watched the momentum of this movement grow, and I watched the impact people made.

It was powerful. For every challenge in every community, it seemed like someone was out there trying to solve it. I decided that this organic approach to change, one that gave ordinary folks the power to do good in the world, was just what we needed in education. If local people could develop local solutions to challenges in their countries and communities, we certainly could give that same opportunity and power to teachers. As an outcome of that idea, Darcy and I created an organization called The Educators' Lab. Since its creation, we've designed new ways to go about professional learning and provided an outlet for teachers to explore education topics that are relevant to the well-being of our students, but that often get ignored.

The Startup Teacher Playbook is a way to grow the same movement we saw in the startup world in the education world. We've provided tools and strategies in this book for you to get your ideas off the ground. You don't need us beyond that. Run your own workshops, get together to go over the Canvas, and support educators who want to solve problems and improve education. We're passing over the reins and can't wait to see what you come up with.

Make the Case: Trust Us to Do Our Jobs

So far, we've shared our frustration with the current state of professional learning, outlined our vision for teachers, and explained how the work of social entrepreneurs can help revolutionize PD and empower teachers. If you've picked up this book, you are a visionary, and you're likely ready to help us make innovation and problem-solving more of a norm in the education space.

Our Ask: Help us make education what it should be: a system where we trust and encourage the professionals trained in teaching and learning (teachers) to do their jobs. A system in which we equip educators to actively address challenges in classrooms and schools and design learning experiences based on the needs of their students. Help us prove to the world what we're capable of when given the opportunity.

Your Role: Help us redefine what it means to be a teacher by solving problems and bringing your ideas to life. Rather than the current reality of being micromanaged and PD'd to death, we want *you* to be confident that you can make changes—big and small—in the best interests of students based on your expertise as an educator.

> **Share Your Work!** Use #StartupTeacher, go to our website, theeducatorslab.com, and share what you're working on. We can't wait to see it.

Spark a Revolution: Help us start a revolution in how we train teachers and use professional learning time. Through your great ideas and work, you'll make a case for why educators should be at the heart of designing the classrooms of tomorrow. You'll exemplify how practicing the art of innovation could give your students the skills they need for the future in a way no other professional learning program could.

Before you dive into this work, we want to address the elephants in the room. We know you may not always have the authority to choose your own professional learning. We also know not everyone is ready for this revolution. For as much as people say they believe in teachers, it may not be obvious to everyone why we should try this idea, even in the smallest capacity. If you need buy-in from someone else (administrators, parents, colleagues, whomever) before you can get started on these modules, we want to make your life a little easier. Here is ammunition to help justify to others why it's beneficial to encourage *you* to embark on this new journey.

✓ Argument 1: Teachers Help Others See the Big Picture

Think about your classroom. Your lessons. Reflect on how your building and district function.

Are people making decisions that consistently put the needs and interests of students first? Are you empowered to ensure those needs are met? Probably not, and this is one core reason we feel professional learning and training need an overhaul. As a teacher, you *know* exactly what problems are holding your students back, but without permission to address them, everything remains status quo.

When we have PD, or any time when we could work on these issues, it seems we're stuck focusing on test scores, data, and percentages, or how well we know our content. It can often seem like one more thing is added to our plate, when what we could really use is time to address the multitude of problems we already have before us.

Sometimes you just have to shout and stomp your feet (not literally) that we're missing the boat. That we're avoiding dealing with those issues that matter the most.

Let's be real: day-to-day issues can act as major setbacks. When do we deal with them?

- The Wi-Fi's not working. (Students won't be able to take part in the lesson we planned, and we now have to modify on the fly.)

- One student is acting out. (Class is being disrupted for all twenty-four-plus students, and we're not quite sure how to support the one that is acting out.)

- We're not sure what's going on in X's home, but he/she seems a bit off today. (Learning will not take place for that student, and we'll need to find time to call home/speak with this student to figure out what's going on, because we're worried.)

> ### Let's look at COVID-19
>
> Almost overnight, teachers had to adapt to remote learning. They had to figure out how to go about distance learning, how to keep the connection with their students, how to address the inequities highlighted by the pandemic, *and* do this from home—often with their own children to care for (and that's just the tip of the iceberg). And guess what? Teachers exceeded everyone's wildest expectations.
>
> But imagine if teachers had been trained in and encouraged to continuously use problem-solving strategies. Imagine if they were empowered to pivot and adapt learning. Then, instead of top-down mandates outlining how remote learning would happen, what if teachers created plans *(informed by district/school requirements)* specific to their strengths and their students' needs? How might the experience be different? What would you have done?

- Kids' reading and/or math levels are all over the place. (Students need personalized learning to match their abilities, so we need time to differentiate learning.)

- Kids are still coming in without writing utensils, their textbook, paper, or handouts. (They can't learn if they don't have the tools they need, and we're unsure how to help them get organized.)

- We've just been asked to take on a new duty. (We lose even more time to focus on the needs in our classroom.)

- Grades are due. (We feel stuck giving arbitrary scores instead of providing feedback on growth.)

Not only are we not given time to solve the smaller problems relevant to ourselves or our students, it feels like we never get to address the issues that really matter.

Many of our kids are carrying invisible backpacks stuffed, some to overflowing, with:

- Worries about food and shelter

- Lack of support and/or love

- Violence and neglect

- Bullying

- Mental health issues

And they'll soon be entering a world where they face issues like:

- Economic inequality

- Global hostilities

- Systemic racism

- Environmental challenges

- Rampant misinformation

- Changing landscape of work

> Teaching is more than academics. We're developing people, and we want those people to have:
> **Good character**: To guide and support them to thrive.
> **High quality of life**: To be healthy and safe, mentally and physically.
> **Gainful employment**: To be productive and have financial stability.
> **Purpose**: To solve societal challenges.
> **Joy**: Because what's the point of everything else without joy?

As educators, we want students to thrive academically, but ultimately, we also want to know we're equipping them for life. In addition to the overwhelming challenges we face every day, we strive to find windows of opportunity to go beyond content and help develop our students into their potential to be amazing people. It shouldn't be so difficult to carve out nuggets of time to help our students develop themselves; to help them explore their values, to find their purpose, and to experience joy. It shouldn't feel like we have to go the extra mile to incorporate the practical know-how that will help students have a high quality of life or to find meaningful employment. We know learning subject matter alone isn't enough to guarantee their well-being, and we need permission to help them deal with the myriad of issues they're facing.

Everyone has good intentions, but we have enough on our plates. We all know one-size-fits-all (curriculum, PD, testing) doesn't work. We all know what we need to do as educators; we just need a chance to do it. While we appreciate the "help," the micromanaging, the fads, the testing, and the data have taken us further off course than we ever could have imagined. We need permission to innovate and to problem-solve. It's the *only* way we can tackle those problems, big and small, that prevent schools from being what they could be.

Argument 2: We're Not "Just" Teachers; We're Learning Designers

Teaching is the profession that leads to all other professions. It's not a job for anyone. We are preparing the next generation to go out into the world and thrive, and as such, we all need to view it with way more prestige. Unfortunately, we've found ourselves in this interesting conundrum where people with zero years of experience in the classroom sometimes have the authority to tell us how to do our jobs, and it's proven to be counterproductive.

Educators live in a unique reality where people *think* they know what teachers do because (almost) everyone sat in a classroom for twelve-plus years. However, their perception of teaching and the *reality* of teaching rarely intersect. Sitting in a classroom doesn't allow you to comprehend the art of teaching and the amount of work it requires. Most people view teachers as transmitters of information, the sage on the stage leading learners through facts and figures which students will regurgitate on a series of tests to then be measured and ranked. But that outdated picture—perpetuated in movies and TV shows and cartoons—is far from the current reality of education.

What People Think Teaching Looks Like:

teacher noun

teach·er | \ `tē-chər \

Definition of *teacher*

One that teaches; especially one whose occupation is to instruct

What Teaching Actually Looks Like:

learning designer noun

learn·ing de·sign·er | \ `lər-niŋ di-`zī-nər 🔊 \

Definition of *learning designer*

1 : someone who acts as a facilitator, coach, synthesizer, counselor, and problem solver

2 : one who designs for and leads young people on their educational journey

To us, the roadmap to a more student-centered education system is clear: reclaim the status of teachers so we can solve problems. We realized that the visionaries were the ones who understood what teachers do, and that we needed to get other folks up to speed to ensure teachers get adequate training and support for doing their jobs to the best of their abilities.

When others define our work as an antiquated practice, it prevents us from meeting our own potential as educators. Many schools, districts, and organizations have put a box around what professional learning should look like because they still have an old-school view. There still seems to be a top-down need for control over what takes place in the classroom, for fear we might get it wrong. Movements like Edcamp and organizations like Donors Choose have proven that teachers can do *so* much more when given the opportunity. When they are empowered, teachers have the capacity to be the best innovators in education.

Since some people use the word "teacher" to mean the sage on stage, we decided on a more accurate description for teachers: *learning designers*. Learning designers are those who act as facilitators, coaches, synthesizers, counselors, and problem-solvers who design and lead young people on their educational journeys. They model the type of thinking and doing they hope to cultivate in their students. As learning designers, we must be allowed to design the learning the students in front of us need, including designing solutions to any obstacle—big or small—that impedes learning. So if you're dealing with someone who has the "just a teacher" syndrome, clarify that no, you're actually a learning designer.

Argument 3: Teachers Are the Only Ones Who Can Do What They Do

Teachers play an incredibly important role in the lives of students. In some cases, we're the last line of defense for those who pass through our doors. In case people forget, make it clear that the kids need *you*. You are their champion, their leader. You are in the driver's seat. They need you to see yourself as a learning designer, to think like a social entrepreneur. If that's not convincing enough, here's why educators—you—are in the best position to be the innovators and game-changers our kids need. Know why?

1. Who else?

Politicians? "Experts" who have never met our students, maybe never been in a classroom (as an adult)? No, it has to be us. While the drums of change have been beating for years now, and great changes are happening in education, they can't come quickly enough. By the time a fix is crafted and handed down from on high for one problem, dozens more emerge and need solutions. Plus, typical one-size-fits-all solutions don't work in education. Local problems frequently require solutions designed for their local context.

Don't get us wrong. Outside experts, academic researchers, and consultants can provide invaluable insight and expertise to help inform and shape our responses to challenges. All have key roles to play in revolutionizing education. But we don't have time to wait. Teachers are in the trenches and have the power to make immediate changes. You know your kids. They are your why, and you are their hope.

2. Teaching (methodology) has the greatest impact on learning outcomes.

Economists Abhijit Banerjee, Esther Duflo, and Michael Kremer won the 2019 Nobel prize for their research on tackling global poverty. They discovered that by breaking down what causes poverty and asking more precise questions, like how specific healthcare or education policies could improve outcomes, countries could take more intentional strides in alleviating poverty. One outcome of this work we found particularly interesting was the importance of high-quality teachers. The trio found that "neither more textbooks nor free school meals made any real difference to learning outcomes. Instead, it was the **way that teaching was carried out that was the biggest factor**" (emphasis added). We took that to heart. By focusing on better training for teachers and emphasizing best practices, we can make the greatest gains for students.

3. We've tried everything else. It hasn't worked.

Each year, $8 billion is spent on professional development in the US, with no evidence it has improved learning outcomes for all students (as reported in The New Teacher Project). Sure, schools have made changes, tried ideas, and hopefully even achieved gains, but nothing suggests we should continue to do what we're doing. Let's save money on the fads and consultants and put our money into ourselves, the teachers, as a potential solution that hasn't been tried yet.

4. We care.

Yes, others care about education too. Involve them. But it starts with us. We have empathy and insights into our users—our students—that others don't have,

because we see students as individuals with potential, not just numbers. We see them as a collective group and know their needs both as individuals and as a cohort. We see them eight hours a day, five days a week, as they struggle and thrive, and as they try, succeed, and fail. We see them in ways big and small that others—even their parents/guardians—sometimes don't see.

5. We know the problems and have solutions.

Because we care and take time to know them, we also hear the complaints from students, parents, and colleagues about what's not working. We see the gaps and frustrations. We know technology isn't the panacea for all educational woes. We know many problems in education have less to do with content and more to do with challenges outside the classroom. We know that what works for student A may not work for student B, but also might not work for student A tomorrow. We constantly remix our lessons, adapt content, and build connections to best serve the needs of those in front of us. We're natural problem-solvers, and we know what students need.

6. Our impact is immense.

Think of all the faces in front of you each day. The faces in the hallway, at practice, rehearsal, club, lunch, recess, or via remote learning. The relationships you build are powerful, and the ripples extend far beyond your classroom. You have a direct impact on so many kids, and that impact compounds like interest.

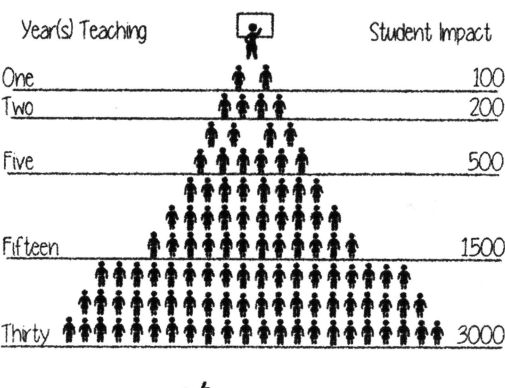

7. These are the skills students need.

We can only transmit what we have ourselves. If we expect to prepare students for the future—to nurture their emotional intelligence, cultivate 21st century skills, and instill entrepreneurial thinking—we need to model those same skills.

8. It saves time in the long run.

While it sounds ambitious, if we get into the habit of tackling issues head on— and starting small is okay!—it will become a natural part of our work. Once we practice and develop a clear system for solving challenges, it will become second nature, and we will save all kinds of time that we would have spent dealing with the repercussions of those problems.

9. Reignite our joy for teaching.

Teacher turnover rates are high, and burnout is an all-too-real problem for many. The reality is that teaching is hard and has become increasingly complicated with every new demand or initiative placed on teachers. So much of teaching feels out of our control. We as teachers need, now more than ever, to take back our classrooms and rekindle our reason for becoming teachers in the first place.

Because (*and here's the kicker*) . . .

10. If you don't treat us like the professionals we are; if you don't give us the space, time, and flexibility to do our jobs, we'll probably end up leaving the classroom.

What'd we miss?
Add your "why teachers, why now" here:

What You'll Get From This Book

We don't promise we can fix education or that we have all the answers. In fact, we don't know if we have *any* of the answers! But we know that *you* do. Through countless workshops with hundreds of teachers crafting solutions to everyday problems, we've seen absolute magic happen. We've seen frustrated teachers rekindle their spark for teaching. We've seen teams develop personalized plans for struggling students. We've watched teachers make simple but deeply meaningful tweaks to lessons, units, and activities. And we've witnessed thoughtful application and implementation of district mandates.

What You Gain from This Process

This book is a vision of how we think these principles can be applied to the education space.

We wrote it because:

- Teachers possess qualities that make them natural problem-solvers. Further developing and honing those qualities is a key factor in project success.

- The process works. When given time (and credit) to craft solutions, teachers are amazing at getting stuff done! You deserve this.

- Being able to work alone is great; being able to galvanize and lead others—be it students, colleagues, or the community—can revolutionize a classroom, school, or community.

We've also seen ...

We've also seen the impact that reclaiming your PD and owning your ideas can have on teachers and schools. You gain:

A system to capture and ignite ideas

Build trust. Build Teams.

Provide role model; build relationships with students

A FAST, efficient process to help you problem solve and achieve goals.

Increase productivity.

Gain and strengthen your own skillset

Chance to PRACTICE what you PREACH. Walk the talk.

Improved learning for greater student success.

Maximize PD time

Personalized solutions to problems

A change in mindset

Increase purpose, job satisfaction, joy

This is our way of giving support and providing coaching to all of the great teachers we've met along our journey who have amazing ideas on how to better serve their students. Taking what we've learned from the startup scene, we hope that our educator version of startup methodology can provide you with insights around innovating so nothing holds you back.

Whether you've been teaching for twenty years or twenty months, the sections of this book will help you build on, hone, and refine the skills you already naturally possess as an educator. Take the ideas that serve you, and leave those that don't. Skip around. Complete a chunk and test the ideas in your classroom. Or read the whole thing. There is no wrong way to use this book.

Each section will help you practice a skillset and develop the mindset we've found helps promote problem-solving and innovation. We also provide coaching and activities designed to address issues that tend to slow down, stymie, stop, or even prevent problem-solving from taking place. The steps in this book are designed to overcome those obstacles and help you. Use them as needed.

You probably already have ideas in mind that you'd like to try, or issues you'd like to solve. If you're new to the innovation process, we recommend reading this book from start to finish. If you're a veteran, feel free to skip to those sections most relevant to you. As a recap, here's what you can expect to gain from each section.

Module Two: Startup Your Ideas: Use the Educator Canvas to Activate Your Ideas and Create the Educational Experiences Your Students Deserve

Teachers diagnose and address problems. Every. Single. Day. For some of us, this comes naturally; for others, a little structure might be nice. The bigger the problem, the more structure we may need. Unfortunately, we are often left to figure things out alone. There's no time or training devoted to helping us solve issues that are holding us back. The biggest obstacle preventing most educators from innovating is simply a lack of tools for implementation. *The Startup Teacher Playbook* provides simple, concrete project management tools to give structure to your ideas and ensure their implementation.

This part of our process is all about helping you get organized and focus on what you want to accomplish. We created the Educator Canvas to provide structure, guiding questions, and clear tasks to support you from problem to solution. The more you do the process, the more natural it will become. This section provides several versions of the Educator Canvas, scaffolded to serve you no matter where you're at in your innovation process.

Module Three: Startup Your Leadership Skills: Build Relationships and Engage Others in Your Work

No teacher is an island. Virtually everything in education revolves around the relationships we build with others. How you run your classroom, how you solve problems, and the projects you create partly depend on how you work with other people. Relationships, relationships, relationships. Being a successful teacher depends so much on how we build relationships with others and how we work with them. This section outlines activities you can do (for yourself or with others) to bolster your skills when it comes to relationships.

So much research is out there about how to be a better leader, and teachers are leading every day. Running a classroom—just like running a business—is not about managing; it's about leading. If you want results, if you want a good workplace or a good classroom, it's about building relationships and setting a clear course so everyone can follow you.

Module Four: Startup Your Mental Stamina: Self-Care Strategies to Prevent Burnout

Teaching is hard. Solving problems can be downright draining. This section is all about your well-being. No one can manage projects or solve problems or innovate if they're exhausted. Self-care goes a long way to decreasing burnout and increasing productivity and project success. As we've worked with teachers, we've noticed that those who grow and thrive often exhibit five basic qualities: Heart, Optimism, Curiosity, Confidence, and Vulnerability. Similar to social entrepreneurs, teachers need time to nurture those qualities so they have the mental stamina they need to see a project through.

Module Five: Professional Learning Resources, Tools, and Strategies to Take Your Ideas to the Next Level

Need more ideas to help you brainstorm? Want to get professional development credit or recertification hours for innovating? Module Five will offer you a path forward.

The book is meant to be visual. It's meant to be applied. Treat it as an opportunity to materialize your ideas. Again, read this book from start to finish if you're looking for more structure; skip around if you're only interested in certain parts. Adapt anything we've created as much as you want. We just want you to *try*. Use the modules that are helpful to you and your goals. Run with it.

And if you fail (okay, *when* you fail), it's okay. We're supposed to be teaching our students how to take risks, how to learn from mistakes, and how to foster a growth mindset. Don't be scared to take risks yourself. We'll be here to catch you if you fall.

We are not here to give you answers, but to help you find the answers you already have within you. When you get stuck, as most people do when trying to make things better, we're here for you.

Reach out:
Via Twitter: #StartupteacherPLN
#Startupteacher
Via Facebook: Educator Lab
Via E-mail: info@educatorlab.io

Final Thoughts

You didn't go into teaching for the money or the fame (as if!). You became a teacher to make a difference, to change lives. For you, it's all about the kids. As teachers, we are in the best position to see what's preventing students from achieving their potential. And crappy PD days, pointless meetings, ridiculous protocols, and endless testing are not going to solve the challenges facing our students.

You are.

You have students' best interests at heart. You know them. You know what they need. You have the solutions. You have the know-how. What you need is the support. That's what this book is for. So even if we can't control or change the whole system (yet), let's take control of what we can, kick some butt, and make the changes we crave—and students need!

Continuing to do things the way they've always been done just won't cut it. We need you—and all the teachers like you—to rethink your role as a teacher and make problem-solving a natural part of your classroom, school, and life.

This is your playbook to problem-solve your own PD so you can do the work that inspires you and best supports your students.

Ready?

Your students are waiting.

You became
a teacher
to make a
difference,
to change lives.

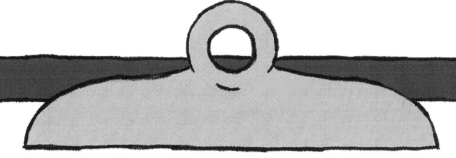

Module Two:

Startup Your Ideas

Use the Educator Canvas to Activate Your Ideas and Create the Educational Experiences Your Students Deserve

In this module:

- The story behind the Educator Canvas tool
- What will you try?
- An example of the Educator Canvas
- Ready to go? How to use the Educator Canvas
- A cheat sheet
- Deep dives: A workbook for your ideas
  - ▶ Articulate the problem: Deep dives to craft your challenge question
  - ▶ Outline your vision: Deep dives to discover your solution
  - ▶ Get focused: Deep dives to articulate your impact
  - ▶ Gain perspective: Deep dives to capture insights
  - ▶ Get organized: Deep dives to outline your logistics
  - ▶ Be prepared: Deep dives to maximize your execution
- Final thoughts

The Story Behind the Educator Canvas Tool

We talk about running your classroom like a startup, but what do we mean exactly?

In Module One, we talked about how you could use basic business fundamentals to break down and identify areas that you could improve in your classroom or school. We emphasized the need to view your classroom as a separate entity from yourself, something you could operationalize and assess for impact. We discussed viewing yourself as a learning designer—the person in charge of designing the educational experiences for your students. But what comes next? What do you actually *do* when you see or hear a challenge? How do you fix problems or design new experiences?

Just as social entrepreneurs use tools to think through challenges within their startups, we are giving you a tangible tool to help you adapt teaching and learning as the need (or inspiration) strikes.

In a space that's fairly risk-adverse, we need a tool that gives us permission to *try,* to take healthy risks for the sake of our students. Startup methodology enables social entrepreneurs to quickly test ideas to see what works (or not) so their startup can move forward (or not). Too often, we as teachers can see what's not working, we know what needs to be fixed, but if we can never try, we can never improve. Instead of letting all those good ideas go to waste, now's your chance to test out your theories.

Hence the Educator Canvas—a project management tool to help turn frustrations into actionable projects and bring good ideas to fruition. This one-page "living document" is designed to help you work through challenges so you, too, can test out solutions and see what could work (or not) for your classroom or students. Inspired by the Business Model Canvas, the Educator Canvas includes a series of questions that guide you through any project, big or small, solo or team, for your classroom or with your class. It's a place for you to sketch out your ideas, see them, think about the tasks required to accomplish your vision, and then quickly test them out for impact. But unlike a simple blank canvas, the Educator Canvas provides cues to help you get started. It's sort of a mental paint-by-numbers. Color in the boxes and a clear vision of how to address your challenge will emerge.

You may think, *Yes! This all sounds wonderful. I'd love to try out the Educator Canvas, but when? What if my ideas don't work and I waste my time?* We know that it's easy to feel like we don't have time and THE CLASSROOM/SCHOOL IS ON FIRE! But you do have time (*cough cough,* which is why we made that big hurrah in Module One about rethinking PD and meeting time). While it might take a few tries to learn the process, addressing challenges, especially those that feel like uphill battles in the classroom, will save time in the long run because you'll be figuring out how to smooth over those issues. You'll waste less time and have fewer headaches because you will learn how to hit problems head on.

A Note About Time

Having doubts about *when* all of this can happen? Experiencing minor flashes of panic and wondering how you're supposed to do this and take care of everything already on your plate? Please note:

*This does not have to be extra. This process can enhance and support the work you do every day: adding new technology, revamping a lesson plan, or developing a new unit.

*Evaluate the use of time. Use team, level, and staff meetings, and transform inservice days to truly be *in service* to students and problem-solving. Tap into planning and prep time.

*We make time for what matters. By giving time for self-care, innovation, and problem-solving to improve your craft or working with others, you'll be a happier, more productive educator. If we're not using our time to reflect on how to improve ourselves and our craft, what are we doing?

Plus, we hope this process eventually becomes so natural that you don't need the Canvas at all. We know that in the craziness of teaching, it can be overwhelming to balance all the tasks and challenges thrown at you. We hope the Canvas can provide the structure and support that are so critical to helping your ideas take flight, that enable you to *try.*

innovation noun

in·no·va·tion | \ i-nə-ˈvā-shən \

Definition of *innovation*

1 : the introduction of something new

2 : a new idea, method, or device

What Is Innovation?

Beyond the Innovation Cliché

The word innovation has become such a buzzword in education that it has lost its meaning to the detriment of our students. Education is flawed and needs innovation. It's full of problems, but also full of opportunities.

So what is innovation? We define it as *the deliberate application of information, imagination, and initiative to address a problem or create an opportunity. It's generating new ideas or adapting old ones to create value for users.*

Considerations as we discuss innovation:

- Innovation is *not* necessarily doing something big. It could be a small tweak to a process, a simple tool you apply to improve learning.
- It's not necessarily doing something *new*. Finding ways to *implement* existing ideas into your context is innovation in itself.
- Throughout this book, we use problem-solving and innovating side by side, at times interchangeably. Not because they mean the same thing, but because we must do both. So when we use one, please hear both words. How can we solve this problem (using innovative ideas)? How can we innovate (to solve this problem)?

What Will You Try?

Determining what you want to tackle can be the hardest part of the entire innovation process. From our experience, you're usually in one of three categories:

1. You feel like you know *exactly* what you want to work on and are ready to dive in.

2. You have so many ideas flooding your brain that you have no idea which to choose or which problem to focus on.

3. You feel a desire to *do* but are utterly clueless as to *what* or *how*. (FYI, that's okay!)

No matter where you are, know this: The best ideas are those on which you reflect, analyze, and give a clear purpose. Before you jump into the Canvas, we want to give you the best shot at success by encouraging you to be thoughtful with the idea you decide to pursue.

A Quick Note About Problems:

The word "problem" often has a negative connotation, but don't let it. It's just a way of addressing what we'd like to improve or fix. In fact, it doesn't necessarily need to be a problem at all. It could be:

- A challenge or frustration that's impeding teaching and learning;

- An area you'd like to improve (for yourself, for your students, for your colleagues);

- A process that would make your life or teaching easier or more successful;

- Something someone suggested (maybe your students) or required (maybe a district mandate), and you want to nail it.

> ### But What If I Fail?
>
> If you are a tad nervous about embarking on all this, please know there's no such thing as failure when you're actively trying to solve problems. You have nothing to lose and everything to gain by trying to improve teaching and learning.
>
> We ask our students to take risks and build a growth mindset, and we need to model the behavior we hope to cultivate in our students. It's all about trying, learning, and failing forward. When we know better, we do better. You're already awesome because you're taking risks and trying. The worst case scenario is not so bad: You may discover another way that won't work.
>
> It's all about perspective. As Confucius said, **"The man who says he can and the man who says he cannot are both correct."**

In Module One, we gave you an example of using business fundamentals to think through how you might break down your classroom operations and uncover what you'd like to address. This is a great way to define and clearly articulate your problem. You can reflect and jot down your thoughts in the space just ahead. You can think through the issues holding you back in the classroom or the problems everyone's complaining about in the staff room. You can also think about what energizes you, or what new ideas you've learned from colleagues or at a conference that you'd like to put into play. As you uncover more and more "problems," we're confident you'll naturally gravitate toward the perfect project for you (and your students).

A Quick Note About Possibility:

Since we don't expect you to immediately know what to do to address a problem, nor do we want you to jump to a solution, let's talk about possibilities. You have countless opportunities to make change, often more than you think! It's okay to start small; it's okay to reinvent. In no way, when we talk about innovating, do we mean getting rid of what is working or starting from scratch.

We've noticed that when teachers talk about problems, they're often talking about big problems, the ones that make us feel powerless or overwhelmed. For instance, we hear educators talk about issues like student engagement or equity or parental involvement. Because of their enormity, they can make us feel like we need to do something huge to fix it all. We don't expect you to fix it all, and you can avoid putting that pressure on yourself. Do what is manageable and relevant to you and your students. Big problems don't necessarily require big solutions, so we want to remind you of all that is *possible* because you can do so much that is within your reach.

Based on our work with teachers and similar work with Changemaker School Districts by Ashoka Youth Venture, most teacher-powered solutions tend to fall into five main buckets. We include them to help you narrow down your thinking—you can't do it ALL at once. These might help you focus in on what would work best for *your* situation. You can make a difference in so many ways. Use this chart to explore the possibilities you have to create change.

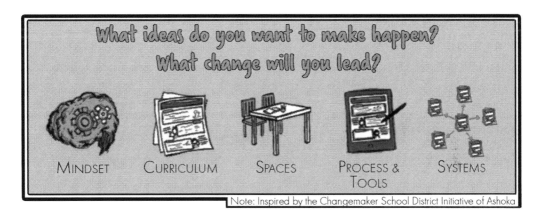

What ideas do you want to make happen?
What change will you lead?

MINDSET   CURRICULUM   SPACES   PROCESS & TOOLS   SYSTEMS

Note: Inspired by the Changemaker School District Initiative of Ashoka

	Mindset	Curriculum	Space	Processes & tools	Systems
Definition	Shifting attitudes and beliefs, creating classroom or school culture	Redesigning lessons, units, activities, and content	Reimagining classroom design, tackling school improvements	Revamping pedagogy; integrating new tools, tech, resources	Overhauling classrooms or school systems, building community
Examples	Cultivating a learning mindset in students, building a culture of gratitude	Creating interdisciplinary lessons, trying new methods (e.g., PBL), or personalizing learning	Starting beautification projects, creating or revamping study and lounge space, designing flexible seating	Integrating new tools for learning, changing up assessment, revamping meeting time	Implementing restorative justice, ensuring equity in the classroom

Use the next couple of pages to explore—mentally—all the opportunities that lay before you. Whether they're problems or possibilities, you can start to uncover what you want to do next. Then, use the Educator Canvas to give it a try.

Problems on My Mind

Issues

Frustrations

Complaints

Classroom Operations

Possibilities on My Mind

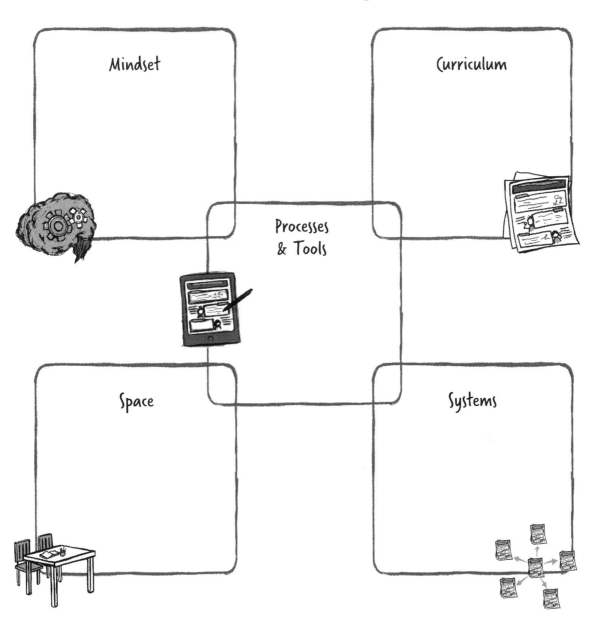

Mindset

Curriculum

Processes & Tools

Space

Systems

An Example of the Educator Canvas

Before you get started on the Canvas, here's an opportunity to see what this tool looks like in action. Take it with a grain of salt as it's just *one* example of what the Canvas can help address. As we've worked with teachers, we've never seen any two Canvases look the same. Even similar problems yield different solutions, as everyone is working and living in a unique context. Think of your students, your school, your district, your colleagues, your administrators, the opportunities available to you, the constraints holding you back—no one else has exactly the same story. We know you'll personalize the Canvas based on *your* needs and scope.

Getting Started: You and Your Team Have Encountered a Problem

Here's the deal … you and your teaching team have had it up to your necks. The kids have been flat-out wild this year, and while you don't know what to do, you agree you have to do something. No matter what you've tried so far, students seem distracted (not interested in content, behavior issues, overall decreased engagement), and teaching and learning just don't seem to be taking place. You decide to get together and put the Canvas to use.

Step 1: Understanding the PROBLEM

Your team meets a few times to dig deep into why this is happening, and decides to do a quick root-cause analysis of the situation.

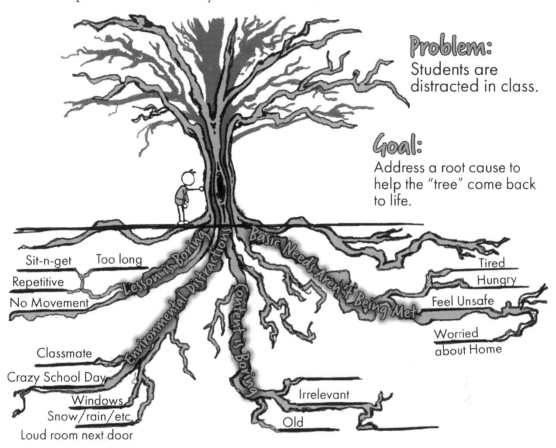

Problem:
Students are distracted in class.

Goal:
Address a root cause to help the "tree" come back to life.

Sit-n-get   Too long
Repetitive
No Movement

Lesson is Boring
Environmental Distractions
Basic Needs Aren't Being Met
Content is Boring

Tired
Hungry
Feel Unsafe

Worried about Home

Classmate
Crazy School Day
Windows
Snow/rain/etc.
Loud room next door

Irrelevant
Old

Your analysis: Students have little to no real buy-in of school or education as a whole, and the curriculum feels irrelevant to their reality.

Your team develops three main challenge questions from your analysis:

Write your Challenge Question

How might I/We ___ACTION___ + ___USER___ + ___IMPACT___ ?

CHALLENGE QUESTION

- How might we ensure students believe school is a pathway for success?
- How might we revamp the curriculum so students are more engaged in learning?
- How might we create a team-wide incentive structure so students have the same behavior expectations across the board?

Step 2: Articulating the SOLUTION

Your group decides to focus on Challenge Question #2. You each feel this is the place where you can make the greatest impact the quickest. Yes, it will be high in effort (you're revamping a whole unit mid-year), but you know it's critical.

PROBLEM

Write your problem as a single statement or question.

How might we revamp the curriculum so students are more engaged in learning?

You set a deadline to come together to brainstorm a solution. Prior to that day, you each get student input about how to approach the challenge. In addition, you each investigate the challenge in your own way, such as reading blogs, asking other teacher friends, or seeking help on Twitter. You agree to bring all the ideas and student input to your brainstorming session.

During the session, you all acknowledge that while you are stuck with some of the content, you definitely have opportunities to build skills and create a more hands-on approach to learning. You decide to start with one unit and see how you might combine content to create a thematic interdisciplinary unit together to meet necessary standards. You feel that by powering up your lessons and working together, you can get students interested in learning and reduce the behavior issues. You work together to create your solution statement.

SOLUTION

Write your theory of change: What do you plan to do and what will that accomplish?

We will create a thematic interdisciplinary unit that meets all necessary standards while connecting to and integrating student interests.

Now you're ready to think through implementation and work through the rest of the Canvas.

Conclusion: Implementation Complete!

Your team creates a superhero-themed unit: Are You a Hero? As a kickoff, students watch a video (Bond-style) telling them an evil villain wants to destroy the world, and it is up to them to save it. Using this theme, each teacher connects their content to the overarching idea of being a superhero, focusing on core ideas that connect to the theme. You make plans to celebrate the end of the unit with a superhero celebration, at which students will share, present, and/or display artifacts of their superpowers in learning.

As you and your colleagues work through the theme and put your own spins on it, each teacher is able to implement the solution in a way that works for his/her classroom, style, and time restrictions. Some connect existing content to the superhero theme, and others craft new superhero PBLs. Everyone feels ownership because they implemented the idea in their own way, and now you can compare outcomes.

A PBL Note: Inspired by your work with the Canvas, you decide to use it with your class for your superhero PBL. It's perfect. You give them the problem to solve, they use activities to devise solutions, and the Canvas helps them implement their ideas. You're able to coach them because this is a tool you use too.

Because you gave the whole school community an overview of your project and goals, others are able to get in on the act. The PE teacher utilizes the PE class to do spring yard clean-up for senior citizens and those in need (raking is, after all, a lot of exercise). They accept donations for their work, and the funds go toward your final celebration. The band teacher adds a superhero-themed song medley to the spring concert and agrees to have students play it to kick off your superhero celebration.

PROBLEM

Write your problem as a single statement or question.

How might we revamp curriculum so students are more engaged in learning?

Project Name

Superhero Interdisciplinary Unit

Short-Term Goals

What would success look like?
How might you measure your goals?
How is your project creting value for others?

- We will see students engaged in the learning process:
  - Increased focus during activities
  - Better marks
  - Positive atmosphere
  - Smiles!
  - Fewer behavior issues
- Measures:
  - observation
  - occasional anonymous exit tickets seeking specific feedback
  - Reflection: end-of-unit short write—by students and teachers—about the value of the work.

 What do you hope to see, hear, feel?
How will you know you're 'successful'?
How will you measure 'success'?

Inspiration

What evidence can you find to validate that this idea could work?
What tools or strategies could you use to adapt to help you implement?

- Learned about a few micro-schools that use guiding question + theme to create an interdisciplinary approach.
  - What's our through-line in what we're teaching and how could make our work align?
- Investigating project-based learning—curious about how teachers assess work. Some Ts not up for that now.
- Looking into gamification. How can we turn learning into a fun challenge?

 You may not use all of your inspiration, but these ideas help stir the pot. Plus, you might not use them now but may later.

Long-Term Vision

Is this a one-off project or a piece of a bigger picture?
How do short-term goals fit into a longer-term vision?

- Believe learning is interdisciplinary and we should teach that way. Aligns with our philosophy.
- Believe students learn best when it's hands-on and applied. Aligns with philosophy.
- We want to have the unit prepared for roll-out 4th Quarter. At the end of the unit we will evaluate how well this strategy worked and retool from there.
- If this goes well, we want to revamp all of our units so they're more engaging, relevant, and interdisciplinary.

Your team outlines the big-picture plan, ensuring that the overall plan connects to each team member's core beliefs and making plans for next steps.

User Input

How will you get buy-in from your user?
How do you plan to get feedback on your solution from your user?

- Survey and Interview Students:
  - Ask kids: What interests you?
  - INPUT: Kids seemed to get really into the superhero theme. Also, feel like they sit for too long; want to go outside more.
- Additional ?s: How will we tie the superhero theme to each subject? Can we get them outside and out of their seats more to make them happy? For those kids who weren't into superheroes, what's our strategy to keep them connected?

 As you get input on your initial solution, you may go back to your user for ongoing input as you flesh out your plan.

IMPACT   INSIGHTS

SOLUTION

Write your theory of change: What do you plan to do and what will that accomplish?
We will create a thematic interdisciplinary unit that meets all necessary standards while connecting to and integrating student interests.

Tasks

What tangible things do you need to produce for this to happen?
What are your concrete next steps and who is accountable for each?
Which tasks could you pass on to others outside your team?

- Create unifying activities that go with theme:
  - 007 style call-to-action video: Are you a hero?
  - Letter from a villain: obstacle
  - Letter from agency: urgency
- Outline of final sharing 'celebration' project requirements
- Invitation to parents/community

 This list will grow and evolve as you work. Having a separate task doc or spreadsheet can help as you add and delete to-dos.

Timeline

Which tasks have the highest priority?
When does each task need to be completed by?

Initial entry: (Early January)
- Meet in two weeks with implementation input from students and our solo 'research.'

Added details: (Late January)
- Brainstorming session on how to use our curriculum with this theme. Bring standards and ideas—two weeks.
- Implement unit 4th Quarter

 NOTE:
Since this is a living document, details will continually be added or evolve as you go.

Resources

What key inputs do you need to complete your task?
- Space   - Tools   - Funding   - Expertise

- Space: For the final sharing celebration, we will talk with admin about ideas and how to schedule.
- Expertise: Schedule our tech coach for a planning session to discuss tech integration and presentation options.
- Funding: Rent-a-superhero fundraiser? Kids do service projects for donations?

 Resources:
Think logistics and planning. Your needs will evolve as you work!

Strategy

How are you going to obtain your resources?
List three things that might go wrong with your plan and how you will overcome.

- Teacher X will definitely cause some push back. We will seek her out as part of our inspiration gathering.
- Will reach out to parents re: superhero costumes for a fundraiser
- Will also ask the local community theatre if we can hold the celebration there.

 Thinking through the roadblocks, including people, can help you plan for success.

Partners

How will you engage needed stakeholders with the project?
How will you pitch your idea to others?
Who would enhance this project?

- Pitch: Share problem and solution statement, focusing on student voice and increasing overall joy/buy-in.
- Parents/Guardians/Community: Recruit local everyday heroes to share their stories. (Could become part of the project.
- We'll use our school social media (with approval) to share our vision

 Partners:
Who can take this project up a notch?
Not your team, but an invested party.

Managing Relationships

What's each team member's role and how will you communicate?
Can you set up a designated spot and time to work?
How might your solution impact others and how might you manage change or stress?

- Tasks are listed—with deadlines—and assigned in our shared spreadsheet.
- Weekly team meetings will be used to discuss action items and progress.
- Others: We'll craft an email overview for colleagues and invite admin to our next meeting. We'll emphasize the potential community connections and authenticity.

By informing everyone, you discover the PE teacher is adding "superhero training" to her plans and wants to do spring cleaning for seniors in PE.

LOGISTICS

EXECUTION

Ready to Go? How to Use the Educator Canvas

STOP The rest of this section acts as a how-to guide for the Educator Canvas. It's your personal coach that will model and support you as you design your project and go from idea to implementation.

As such, if you're not reading through this section in tandem with the Canvas, it can quickly get overwhelming. The parts of this section directly correlate to the boxes of the Canvas, helping you to think deeply about each area of implementation. You can read straight through, but if you don't have a project in mind, the content may feel irrelevant. That's okay. Feel free to skim through to get a general understanding, or read the topics relevant to your project, or skip to the wrap-up on page 130. We'll meet you there.

 Now that you have an idea in mind, it's time to get to work. Look a couple pages ahead and come right back. You'll see the Educator Canvas and can get a quick feel for what it looks like. Feel free to make a copy or download it at theeducatorslab.com. It will be helpful to look at the Canvas while you read the book.

That's it. Looks super simple, right?

On the one hand, the Canvas is simple. It will guide you through your idea, forcing you to ask yourself the questions you need to consider to implement your idea.

On the other hand, it can feel overwhelming. We get it. It takes time to solve problems, and sometimes the bigger the problem, the more complex and time-consuming the solution and implementation process can be.

Whether or not you're new to the innovation space, take a shot at it. You can fill it out in this book, download it online and print it, or make a copy. You can also use Post-its, open up a Google Doc, or hash out the questions from the Canvas in any way that works best for you.

This is not a traditional organizer to be neatly completed box by box—although we'll do our best to guide you through as you read this section. As a living document, it's meant to generate conversation and help you flesh out ideas, so it's completely normal to find yourself thinking, circling back, jumping around, deleting, and revamping as you move through it. This is not a linear process. Expect to bounce back and forth between boxes as your idea evolves.

Also, there's no right way to do this. We don't care if you use complete sentences; we just want you to be able to write it out, draw it out, and get those ideas down in whatever form works best. You can do the Canvas with anyone. We encourage you to use it with colleagues, parents, and students.

Take your time. Most of these challenges aren't going anywhere, so do what you can, when you can. The worst-case scenario is that you push too hard, too fast, and get burned out, then stop trying altogether. That's not helpful for anyone. So take breaks as needed. This will likely take longer than you think (at least the first few go-rounds). Embrace the opportunity to revise and revisit and redo pieces as you go.

Ready to give it a whirl? We invite you to get started. You can do this!

Or if you're not quite ready to take the plunge solo just yet, check out the Canvas cheat sheet (pages 75–77) and the deep dives (pages 78–129) for more support and guidance.

Mental Note: The Canvas Is Agile in Its Uses

This section focuses on how to use the Educator Canvas to work through and implement your ideas, but feel free to use it for any purpose you see fit. Yes, use the Canvas to make improvements in your classroom (e.g., to incorporate that new tech tool or revamp that one unit), but also use the Canvas beyond your classroom needs. Here are a few additional ways you can use the Canvas:

1. **Staff Support.** An ideal way for instructional coaches or facilitators to organize follow-through in a meeting or workshop.

2. **Idea Generation.** A great framework for admins (or anyone else) who want to capture a brainstorming session.

3. **Student Support.** A perfect tool for any teacher in need of structure for a student project or PBL.

Educator CANVAS

PROBLEM
Write your problem as a single statement or question.

Project Name

Short-Term Goals
- What would success look like?
- How might you measure your goals?
- How is your project creating value for others?

Inspiration
- What evidence can you find to validate that this idea could work?
- What tools or strategies could you use or adapt to help you implement?

Long-Term Vision
- Is this a one-off project or a piece of a bigger picture?
- How do short-term goals fit into a longer-term vision?

User Input
- How will you get buy-in from your user?
- How do you plan to get feedback on your solution from your user?

IMPACT

INSIGHTS

SOLUTION
Write your theory of change: What do you plan to do and what will that accomplish?

Tasks
- What tangible things do you need to produce for this to happen?
- What are your concrete next steps and who is accountable for each?
- Which tasks could you pass on to others outside your team?

Timeline
- Which tasks have the highest priority?
- When does each task need to be completed by?

Resources
- What key inputs do you need to complete your task?
  - Space
  - Tools
  - Funding
  - Expertise

Strategy
- How are you going to obtain your resources?
- List three things that might go wrong with your plan and how you will overcome.

Partners
- How will you engage needed stakeholders with the project?
- How will you pitch your idea to others?
- Who would enhance this project?

Managing Relationships
- What's each team member's role and how will you communicate?
- Can you set up a designated spot and time to work?
- How might your solution impact others and how might you manage change or stress?

LOGISTICS

EXECUTION

A Cheat Sheet

The Canvas gives you a place to start and a way to work through the ideas that burble up in the shower or during your commute home, but that doesn't mean it's easy to turn them into action. Don't feel bad if (when) you get a little stuck.

To help you articulate the different aspects of your idea, we've provided a cheat sheet to guide you on your journey toward implementation. Each piece includes additional probing questions that go deeper into each of the boxes than the Canvas itself, providing you with a bit more instruction and guidance.

This may be enough to send you on your way. Keep working through the boxes and return here when you've done all you can and need help with the next step. If you get stuck at any point, you can use the deep dives in this module for further coaching and assistance. You can also consult the example we provided at the beginning of this module.

As we said before, expect to bounce back and forth between boxes, as everything is interrelated. Completing one box may inspire you to revise another. As your ideas evolve, so will your project!

Finally, we encourage you to show your Canvas to others to further improve your project. Trusted colleagues, mentors, and potential users can provide instant feedback and help ensure the best possible outcome.

Don't overthink it, just keep writing. Kinks will work themselves out as you go.

Come back and read through some or all of the deep dives when you want some additional coaching and support to further develop your boxes. Skip around this section as is most helpful to you and your process. Or meet us in Module Three!

Good luck!

Educator CANVAS

PROBLEM

Write your problem as a single statement or question.

How might I/We _____ ACTION _____ + _____ USER _____ + _____ IMPACT _____ ?

Project Name

Short-Term Goals

What would success look like?
How might you mesaure your goals?
How is your project creating value for others?

- What do you want to achieve and how will this project achieve those goals?

- How will you know if this idea is working? Think through indicators that might demonstrate success.

Inspiration

What evidence can you find to validate that this idea could work?
What tools or strategies could you use or adapt to help you implement?

- What ideas, resources, or practices can you tap into and adapt for your project?

- Who can you reach out to in your building/district, PLN or thru social media for ideas and feedback?

- Can you draw on any research that might prove even a small part of your solution?

Long-Term Vision

Is this a one-off project or a piece of a bigger picture?
How do short-term goals fit into a longer-term vision?

- What might next steps be after this project is complete?

- How does this work fit into your professional goals and educational philosophy?

User Input

How will you get buy-in from your user?
How do you plan to get feedback on your solution from your user?

- How will you get and use feedback from your user (who you're designing for)?

- How would they want you to implement your solution?

IMPACT

INSIGHTS

SOLUTION

Write your theory of change: What do you plan to do and what will that accomplish?

- I/We will _____(ACTION)_____ so (that) _____(IMPACT)_____
- *** This is your North star for what you want to achieve! ***

Tasks

What tangible things do you need to produce for this to happen?
What are your concrete next steps and who is accountable for each?
Which tasks could you pass on to others outside your team?

- How will you organize, track, and update your tasks?
- How can you utilize allies for some tasks?
- What is a need to do vs. a want to do?
- Consider strengths, interests, workload, and what is realistic for each person.

Timeline

Which tasks have the highest priority?
When does each task need to be completed by?

- What's a realistic amount of time to complete each step?
- Think about sequencing: What has to be done before the next steps can occur? What's more flexible?

Resources

What key inputs do you need to complete your task?
- Space   - Tools   - Funding   - Expertise

- Who could you ASK to obtain resources? How can you maximize your community, colleagues, classes?
- What is a need to have vs. a want to have?

Strategy

How are you going to obtain your resources?
List three things that might go wrong with your plan and how you will overcome.

- How can you get creative and resourceful about obtaining your resources?
- What hurdles are at the back of your mind?

Partners

How will you engage needed stakeholders with the project?
How will you pitch your idea to others?
Who would enhance this project?

- Who do you need on your side? Who do you want on your side? How do those people like to be approached?
- How can you "sell" your ideas to others? What's your one-minute pitch? Why should others support your work?

Managing Relationships

What's each team member's role and how will you communicate?
Can you set up a designated spot and time to work?
How might your solution impact others and how might you manage change or stress?

- Can you each articulate what the other person is going to do, how, and by when? Check each other.
- How might you avoid any drama that could occur with the implementation of your project?

LOGISTICS   EXECUTION

Articulate the **PROBLEM**: Deep Dives to Craft Your Challenge Question

 Write your problem as a single statement or question.

If you're not totally sure *what* you want to work on, read this section! This deep dive will develop your scope of work by helping you craft a challenge question. You can't solve it all at once, so use these next few pages to refine your problem and craft a single challenge question to guide your work. Go to the step that will help you articulate your problem.

> Don't try to solve a *list* of questions; take one at a time!
>
> Here's an overview of the process we use to help educators develop their challenge questions. It's differentiated so you can start wherever works best for you.

Step 1: Decide which problem to focus on: If you're still unsure what to do and have a list of ideas or issues in your head, start on the next page. This activity forces you to analyze your ideas and select the one that you find to be most needed and most practical. Start on page 79.

Step 2: Clearly state your problem as a question: This activity helps you refine your efforts so you clearly articulate what you want to do, who it will help, and how it will help them. Hop over to page 80 to get started.

Step 3: Pick apart your problem to dive deeper: Make sure you're getting to the core of what you need to do with these activities that are designed to help you think critically about your challenge question (again, this will be more helpful if you have drafted a challenge question). NOTE: Depending on the scale of your challenge, you may or may not need this step! If you do, head over to page 82.

Step 1: Decide which problem to focus on

 If you already know the problem you want to work on, please skip ahead to the next page.

You've already had a chance to reflect on problems and possibilities in the previous pages. Using those notes or this activity, start to synthesize your thoughts and sift through them. Bundle the ideas that go together. Prioritize which seem to have the most value or potential impact for your students. Narrow it down to your top three and then select the one that you feel is most feasible and will add the most value.

Getting Started
What do I work on?

What are your most pressing frustrations? (Think big and small)	What are your main goals for this school year? For the next five years?	What's been on your "to-do" list to improve or to try?	What might students, colleagues, or parents say are problem areas?

Funnel Your Ideas
Pick your top THREE areas that ultimately seem to have the most impact on your students.

1)
2)
3)

PICK THE ONE THAT IS MOST NECESSARY AND PRACTICAL

Step 2: Clearly state your problem as a question

You've got your problem, now it's time to turn it into a question. It's not always easy, but it's an important step that helps you define the key aspects of what you'd like to achieve. Turning your problem into a question will help you articulate what you're working on to others, open up dialogue, encourage collaboration, and keep possibilities open as to how you might solve it. Use the examples on the next page as inspiration for what these might look like.

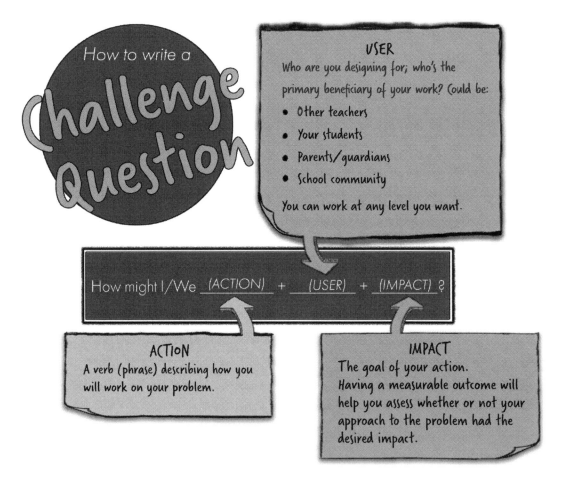

Note: Feel free to adapt the question. Just make sure the key components (Action, User, Impact) are all there.

Give it a try:

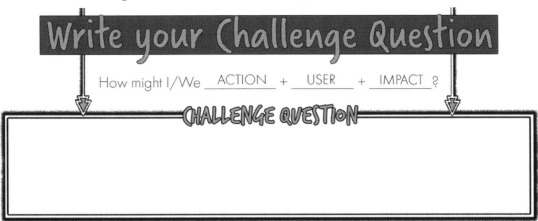

Write your Challenge Question

How might I/We ___ACTION___ + ___USER___ + ___IMPACT___ ?

CHALLENGE QUESTION

Challenge Question Examples

Problem:	Sample Challenge Questions:
Students are distracted in class.	How might I make class more interactive so students are more engaged in learning?
District has mandated a new curriculum/tool you don't like.	How might our level team implement the mandated curriculum/tool in an authentic way to support all learners?
Parents/guardians aren't engaging with school.	How might I use technology to keep parents informed and connected?
Teachers are concerned they don't have adequate prep or time to support students.	How might we revise our bell schedule to give teachers and students more time, or use time more effectively?

Want practice writing challenge questions? What other challenge questions might you write in response to the problems listed above?

Step 3: Pick apart your problem to dive deeper

 This section will make you rethink your challenge question. If you're satis-fied with your question, you may want to skip this part. If you're ready to question yourself—in a positive way—then keep reading.

In order to address any problem, you need to really know the problem. What is happening? When does it happen? Why does it seem to happen? Who is involved and impacted? It's easy to rattle off answers, but if we're honest, there's usually more to our challenges than we can see if we're only looking at the collective image. When we take that image apart and know, really know, what we're working on and who we're working for, we're bound to see new details, new ideas, and new solutions to address our challenges.

Like putting your problem under a microscope, the next few pages are all about examining your problem and learning about it from different angles. We want you to slice it up. X-ray it. Hit it with a magnifying glass. Okay, you get it: We want you to really look at the problem.

Why? Because the best solutions evolve from carefully reflecting upon and ana-lyzing the problem itself. Now it's time for a problem reality check. These tend to be the top four questions we ask when people share their challenge questions with us at workshops. Take a look at your challenge question and see whether it passes this little test. If not, it doesn't mean your question is "bad," it just shows you may need to refine.

Ask yourself:

#1 Is this actually a problem? (or gossip, venting that doesn't warrant action?)

#2 Is the problem's effort worth the potential impact? (impact versus effort check)

#3 Is the problem actually the problem, or are you working on a symptom? (XY problem check)

#4 Is the problem you've identified the problem that needs to be addressed? (root cause analysis)

Activity #1: Is this actually a problem? (Validation)

This is about being honest with yourself and/or getting feedback. If you have a moment, share your challenge question with someone. Do they understand what you want to achieve? Do they agree this is a good challenge to work on? If not, fine tune!

Activity 2: Is it worth the effort?

Where does your question fall on the chart? Adjust as needed.

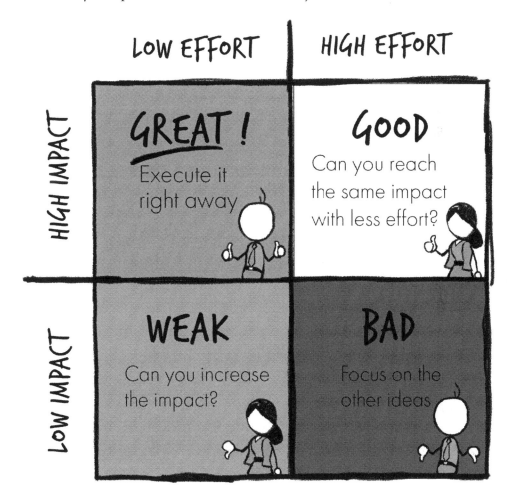

Activity 3: Are you working on the problem or a symptom of the problem?

(Sometimes it's okay to work on the symptom, because that's the best we can do.)

The XY problem (xyproblem.info) is when we are trying to solve a problem, but instead of focusing in on the real problem (because we have no idea how to solve that or even what that is), we focus on a subproblem. Like if you had a burst pipe in your house and spent all your time devising the best way to mop up water (Y) but haven't turned off the water yet (X). We can try to fix Y, but you won't get far until you address the root and solve X.

Take a minute to reflect: Are you working on the X or the Y?

Activity 4: Is it possible for you to go deeper into your problem?

Identifying the best problem to work on isn't always easy. Have you thought through the root causes of the problem? Do you understand why that problem is happening? The deeper you go, the better prepared you'll be to craft a targeted solution. Use the following Root Cause Tree to visually represent your problem and break down its various causes.

- What is the big issue that is preventing your "tree" from growing? Put that on the trunk.

- What are the possible reasons the problem exists? Put those reasons on the large roots. These are all the possible causes for the problem.

- What contributes to those causes? Use the smaller roots that branch out to list what contributes to each cause.

See a completed Root Cause Analysis in the Canvas example on page 65.

Now review: Are you truly addressing a cause of the problem? Does one cause seem greater than the others? One that might be easier to address? One that must be addressed first?

Reflect: Do you need to redefine your challenge?

_____

_____

_____

_____

_____

_____

Challenge Question Evolution: Rewrite and Reword as Needed

How might I/We _____ + _____ + _____?
(ACTION)   (USER)   (IMPACT)

Outline Your Vision: Deep Dives to Discover Your Solution

SOLUTION

Not sure *how* to tackle your problem? That's normal. By slowing down and taking time to think about different solutions, you are forcing yourself to be intentional with how you address your challenge. Your solution statement will act as your North Star for the work you're about to undergo and will help you clearly share what you're trying to do. We encourage you to think deeply and deliberately about your ideas to help you make the best use of your time and energy, which we all know are precious commodities in our line of work. While it may mean more time up front, it will save you time in the long run by ensuring your project has a better chance of success the first go-round.

Read this section if you feel unsure of how to address your challenge question. This is the process we guide educators through when they're trying to explore all their possibilities:

Step 1: Uncovering Potential Solutions: You're undecided on what you'd like to do to address your challenge. You're ready to brainstorm, to consider alternatives, scope out solutions, and think through what's best for your user. Start on page 87 to begin the exploration.

Step 2: Deciding Which Solution to Implement: You've thought of numerous ideas and now it's time to choose which one to develop. We've provided guiding questions to ask yourself and help you determine which solution to pursue. Hop over to page 92 if you're in the process of selecting the solution you want to develop.

Step 3: Creating Your Solution Statements: You know what you want to do. Now it's time to capture your solution into a single sentence. This one-liner will help you clearly articulate your solution to others so they understand what you're going to work on. Head to page 94 if you're ready to craft this statement.

Step 1: Uncovering Potential Solutions

Use this section to expand your mind, get creative, and explore possibilities. These activities will put you back in the learner's seat, helping you discover more about your challenge and what you could do to solve it.

Activity #1: Get the Creative Juices Flowing with a Brainstorming Session

The first step to brainstorming: write it all down. What's already on your mind? What ideas do you already have? Write down any and all ideas—in the box or on a separate sheet of paper. Next, who can you invite to the conversation? Ask your challenge question to others and see what input they have. Ideas will grow as others add to and refine it. So brainstorm—with yourself, with your students, with colleagues, and with anyone whose input you value. Remember: Quantity over quality when getting started.

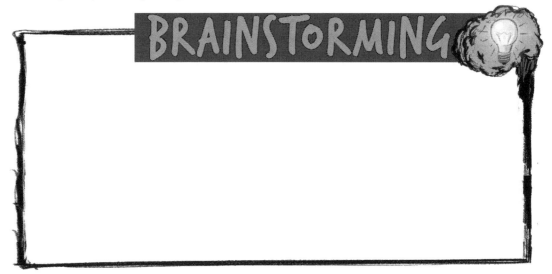

Once you've gotten everything down, take a look at your list. Are you satisfied? If you still want to push your thinking, practice creativity exercises to keep your session going. Use the brainstorming activities (pages 260–265) in Module Five to keep going.

Want more? Practice Design Thinking

Human-Centered Design is one of the best processes to break down challenges and uncover solutions. We highly recommend tapping into their strategies for brainstorming and empathy. Explore the resources from the masters themselves with IDEO's Design Kit.

Activity #2: Investigate: What are other people doing?

There's no harm in tapping into what's already out there. The greatest compliment you can give a teacher is to borrow their great idea. Solutions don't always need to be new. Using great ideas from others to solve your challenge is efficient and effective, and they will still be *your* solutions because *you* will implement them. As we've said before: Innovation does not mean throwing out what works, but it might mean adapting an "old" idea to make it work even better for you and your students.

There's no need to reinvent the wheel! Your solution will be unique because only you know how to implement it effectively for your users. Use the inspiration box to write down ideas, strategies, and tools that speak to you, or go back to your brainstorming page and add the new ideas you've uncovered.

Finding Inspiration:

- Social media: Twitter, Facebook, Instagram, Pinterest (remember, just because it looks good, doesn't mean it is)
- Good ol' Google
- Blogs, vlogs, journals (Cult of Pedagogy, Edutopia, KQED's Mindshift)
- Books (Hack Learning Series)

CONSIDER!

Check out blogs, social media, podcasts, or articles to see how others are tackling this issue. List at least FIVE of your favorite pieces of inspiration.

Inspiration

Activity #3: Give Voice to Your User

Think about your audience: Who is the main recipient or beneficiary of this project? What will they gain from this? Giving your user a voice is one of the best ways to ensure greater problem-solving success. If your user doesn't like the solution, your problem will persist. What *we* think is important can be quite different from what's important to *our user*, which is why it's so critical to consult our users and incorporate their ideas into the solution. Ensuring the user is at the heart of your solution will ensure better results.

Getting Input From Users

Try at least one of these strategies and then write down your findings in the Input box.

- Use an informal survey
- Shadow a student
- Start a suggestion box

- Observe them
- Listen to them
- Interview them
- Talk to them
- Create a class PBL

Tips for User Input

- Meet them where and when they are comfortable.
- Meet them how they are comfortable: in a group or solo, over lunch or over the phone.
- Make the meeting low stress for them. Keep it short, informal, and positive.
- Talk less, listen more. You might not agree with them, but don't let that show.
- Don't judge or argue with them about their responses; just ask open questions.
- Ask clarifying questions as needed (without judgment or comment!).

Synthesize and assess your findings in the following space or on a separate sheet of paper. Add new ideas to your brainstorming box.

CONSIDER!

Share your challenge with students and colleagues. Note their observations and opinions on the matter.

Input

Solutions I Am Pondering:

_____

_____

_____

_____

_____

_____

_____

_____

_____

_____

Step 2: Deciding Which Solution to Implement

We've seen it and experienced it countless times: A flood of possible solutions roils around, and it is both exciting and overwhelming. Perhaps you've received desperate input from users; maybe multiple tools exist that could address your problem. Maybe some ideas just feel "cooler" than others. As we've said before, most problems have *many* possible solutions, and it can feel daunting to know which to choose.

We're here to help. Ask yourself these questions to help you determine the solution you feel best addresses the problem and achieves your goal:

1. Which one best addresses the challenge and is the most possible?

You may have used this box to decide on a challenge, but the same rules apply when thinking through your solution.

2. Which solution would your users greet with the most enthusiasm?

(Hint, hint: ask them!)

3. Which solution best meets your goals?

Jump over to the impact column on the Canvas (pages 98–106) and fill in the boxes.

4. What's within your capacity?

Be realistic, because you're a busy person. What's the solution you feel confident about executing?

We've heard teachers say it'd be best to start from scratch and redesign their school. We hear you! However, that is likely not possible. Instead of doing nothing, focus on what you can do.

Step 3: Creating Your Solution Statements

In the startup world, they often ask you to develop a one-line description of your business (an elevator pitch). They say if you can't describe the value of what you're doing in a single sentence, then you need to keep working on it. We invite you to do the same, as this is a key step toward the successful implementation of your idea. The more specific you can get with your idea, the more achievable and doable it will be. Narrowing down your idea into *one* sentence will not only make it more manageable, but it will also help you to talk about it in concrete

> **Getting stuck?**
>
> Sounds crazy, but draw your solution. It doesn't need to be anything professional. Drawing helps you work out the details. If you can't visualize it, you probably still have a bit more work to do.

terms to others and make it tangible so you can begin the implementation process.

> By writing a couple of solution statements, you may find multiple viable solutions to your challenge. That's great! Just pick and focus on one at a time.

Once you're confident with your idea, try to declare your solution in one sentence. This can be difficult. Take a few stabs at it to ensure you've captured what you want to do and accomplish. It's normal not to get it right on the first go. Flesh it out and continue to break it down into the most basic terms so you can articulate it to others.

I/We will _____ so (that)
_____.

Once you have both your challenge question and your solution statement, try sharing them with another person. Do they get what you're trying to do? Does your solution act as an "answer" to your challenge question? If not, revise.

Solution Statement Evolution: Rewrite and Reword as Needed

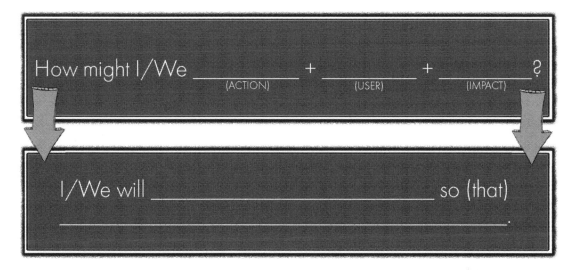

How might I/We _____ + _____ + _____ ?
                     (ACTION)   (USER)   (IMPACT)

I/We will _____ so (that) _____ .

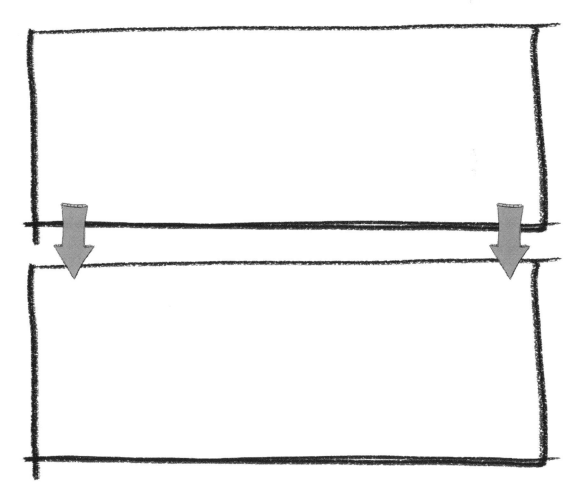

Challenge Question and Solution Statement Examples:

Problem:	Challenge Question:	Solution:
Students are distracted in class.	How might I make class more interactive so students are more engaged in learning?	I will develop a daily learning choice "menu" for independent work time so students can personalize their learning.
		I will integrate three to four learning stations into lessons so students have choice and movement throughout the day.
		I will work with students to incorporate Genius Hour so students can work on a project/learning objective of their choice.
District has mandated a new curriculum/tool you don't like.	How might our level team implement the mandated curriculum/tool in an authentic way to support all learners?	We will use meeting time to personalize the curriculum to best serve the needs of students in our classrooms.
Parents/guardians aren't engaging with school.	How might I use technology to keep parents informed and connected?	We will develop a social media engagement strategy that connects and engages parents/guardians with our classrooms.
		I will pilot (name an app) to message and share resources with parents/guardians to see if engagement increases.
Teachers are concerned they don't have adequate prep or time to support students.	How might we revise our bell schedule to give teachers and students more time/use time more effectively?	We will convene a group of students and teachers to investigate other bell schedules and make a recommendation that administration could follow.

Note: Just as any problem has many possible challenge questions, any challenge question has many possible solutions. If you'd like to practice writing solution statements, use the examples to create your own.

It's normal
not to
get it right the
first go.

Get Focused: Deep Dives to Articulate Your Impact

Summary

You've got your problem and solution down; now it's time to think through your goals and ensure your solution strategically aligns with the impact you seek to create. Use these boxes to develop targets so you put your time and energy into the activities that count. Your solution and impact should go hand in hand. You've used the solution box to explain what you want to do, and now in the impact boxes, you'll explain what your solution should accomplish. As you clearly articulate your goals, don't be surprised if your solution, and the actions needed to achieve it, continues to evolve.

Short-Term Goals

- What would success look like?
- How might you measure your goals?
- How is your project creating value for others?

What impact do you want to make through your work?

Long-Term Vision

- Is this a one-off project or a piece of a bigger picture?
- How do short-term goals fit into a longer-term vision?

> Remember, this is a living document. It will ebb and flow as new information is gathered or comes to life.
>
> Change things as much and as often as necessary.

IMPACT

Use the activities in this section to:

- Define the scope of your work.

- Demonstrate how your project adds value.

- Develop the moving parts of your solution so you achieve your goals.

- Design metrics or indicators to help you validate whether your idea is working.

- Align your project with your educational philosophy.

- Think holistically of what you want to accomplish for your classroom/school.

Activities to Focus Your Short-Term Goals

The Short-Term Goals box forces you to outline the benefits of your project and will be vital when it comes time to evaluate the success of your work. Each goal helps you to set a standard so you know if you're making progress. If you implement your solution and it doesn't meet your goals, you'll know you need to try a different approach (and that's okay).

General Tip:

Think through how this project helps you do what you "have to" do while also putting students (needs, interests, skills) first.

If you're feeling stuck establishing specific goals or figuring out how to assess if you're achieving your goals, here are a few activities to guide you through:

ACTIVITY #1: Draw It

What does success look like? Draw this project in action.

Drawing helps you clearly communicate your why and increase buy-in.

ACTIVITY #2: Get on the Same Page

If you're working with a team, have each team member generate one or two goals, then share them. How similar are your goals? Clarify so you are all on the same page and moving in the same direction.

| Teammate 1 | Teammate 2 | Teammate 3 | Teammate 4 |

> Helps you save time by ensuring everyone's vision is clear.

ACTIVITY #3: Measure It

Make sure you're making progress. List a few indicators to help you assess whether your solution is working. No fancy data necessary, just quick checks that are:

- Measurable: attendance is up, behavior reports are down

- Observable: more smiles, less side chatter, more hands raised

- Validating: user satisfaction such as exit tickets, student/user survey, discussions

Indicators for Success

Indicators:

A specific, observable, and measurable characteristic used to show changes or progress toward achieving a specific outcome.

Activities to Activate Your Long-Term Vision

Here's your space to think big. How could your project fit into your long-term goals as an educator? Do you want to make this a permanent part of your classroom? Are you just testing it out because of curiosity? Establishing your long-term vision is a way to craft clear stepping-stones for your overall purpose as an educator and has three major purposes:

1) Fosters Big-Picture Thinking.

During the school year, it's easy to get laser-focused on what *needs* to be done. The prepping, planning, testing, and grading can start to consume us, and it can feel like we're doing tasks to check off the boxes. Try to make sure that whatever you're working on gives meaning and purpose to you and your students.

2) Defines the Parameters of Your Project.

Pace yourself and establish whether a greater scope for this work exists. Innovation seems to have a snowball effect. The more we do it, the better we get at it. The bolder our ideas become, the easier it is for projects to explode and get out of control. Use this section to set parameters so you stay focused (and sane).

3) Helps to Assess Your Project's Success, Failure, and Next Steps.

With each project, you need to know when to call it quits, either because you've succeeded and your work is done or because your solution didn't work the way you hoped. It's key to know what obstacles are normal and when it's time to move on.

Activity #1: Educational Philosophy

Ensure that what you're working on contributes to your educational philosophy and long-term goals by asking yourself the following questions:

Why do I believe in this project?

How is this project helping me to be the kind of teacher I want to be?

How could this project be a step toward a greater, big-picture goal for my classroom, my school, or myself?

Activity #2: Establish Parameters

Some projects feel small but are actually building blocks to a larger effort. Other projects quickly get out of hand, as it's common to try to do too much at once. As you begin a project, take time and think through how big or small you want the project to be, including outlining possible next steps. Be realistic with your time.

One-and-Done Projects

Let's say you're incorporating a new app or revising a unit. When you're finished, what might be your next steps?

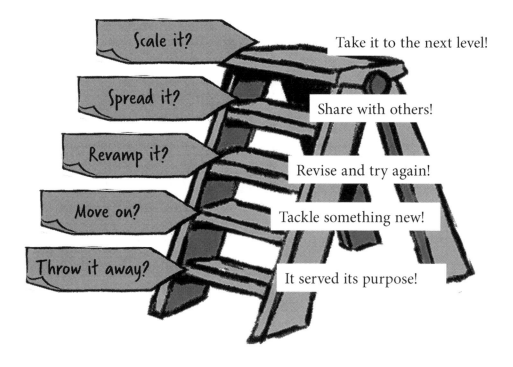

Multi-Phase Projects

Lay out your vision and articulate how this project is a part of a larger puzzle. How will the steps of *this* phase lend themselves to your grand plan?

Parameter Notes

Activity #3: What's Next Analysis

A key component to any learning experience is reflection. As you implement your solution, use the What's Next Analysis to help you assess the good, bad, and ugly of your work. This will help you internalize the Canvas process and make you even *more* successful on your next attempt. (Plus, a lot of projects become the first step or two on a greater quest. If appropriate, lay out what's next.)

What's Next Analysis			
Think about the aspects of your solution that were successful:		**Think about the pieces of your solution that didn't quite work out (or bombed):**	
How can you expand or grow this idea?		What was the first sign things were not working?	
How can you take this idea to the next level or to more users?		What pieces of your solution did work?	
How can you share your success with colleagues and the teaching community?		What did you discover about your problem that might necessitate a different solution?	
Might this solution also help with other problems?		What cause of the problem might you need to address first?	
What factors at your school helped you/your project succeed? (Be sure to thank the people who helped pave the way for you)		What factors (systems, people, traditions, culture, rules) at your school may have impeded your success? Are there ways to address or overcome them?	

Gain Perspective: Deep Dives to Capture Insights

Summary

In order to set up you and your project for success, we want to help you think through two areas we find often get ignored when thinking through implementation: How do we tap into what already exists, and how do we capture student voice (or the voice of your user)? Use the boxes in this section to ensure you implement your idea in the most effective way possible. Even the best ideas can go awry if not launched properly.

We don't believe it makes sense to do more work than you have to, and we know you're more likely to succeed when your user is at the heart of how you implement your ideas. Use the activities in this deep dive to work smarter, not harder, so you can bring your project to life.

Use activities in this section to:

- Ensure you don't reinvent the wheel.

- Ensure your initiative is student-first.

- Enhance your solution by taking advantage of what's already out there.

- Gather feedback from users on how to implement your project so you avoid making assumptions (and wasting time).

- Increase user buy-in to yield greater satisfaction for you and for them.

Inspiration

- What evidence can you find to validate that this idea could work?
- What tools or strategies could you use or adapt to help you implement?

NOTE: Your solution might evolve from doing this section. That's great! It helps ensure you enact the best possible solution the first time. Feel free to rewrite and rework as you go.

User Input

- How will you get buy-in from your user?
- How do you plan to get feedback on your solution from your user?

INSIGHTS

Activities to Foster Inspiration

If you've ever been told it's bad to beg, borrow, and steal ideas, we'd like to counter and say it's a good practice in the innovation space. When it comes to solving problems, we think sharing, adapting, modifying, and revising ideas are often a far better use of time than starting from scratch. Yes, give credit where credit is due, but use the many great ideas that already exist and make them your own! Long story short: There's no shame in tapping into what already exists. We encourage it.

Right now, the education space is oversaturated in the "resources" department; use that to your advantage. Most educators are dying for others to take their resources, use their apps, and apply their research so more students can benefit. The result can still be *your* solution because you can implement others' ideas in a multitude of ways. Save yourself time and enhance your work by seeing how you can use existing resources and ideas.

Activity #1: Hop on Social Media

See what other educators are doing. They've often already made mistakes, so you don't have to. They may have tips, strategies, or tools for how to best implement your solution. Search your topic by hashtag.

New to Twitter? Say hi using the @Educatorslab and/or @dbakkegard handle for a follow. Use the #startupteacher to join our PLN.

What'd you find?

Activity #2: Dig Into the Research and Data

Maybe someone already investigated best practices. Learn from this work to craft the best implementation strategy. Plus, if you need buy-in from other stakeholders (e.g., parents or admin), it's good to have a credible source to back up why your project is worth pursuing. You'll gain this "proof of concept" when you can show that others have found success with similar solutions. The more novel your idea, the less data you'll find to back it up, but you can still find support to explain your need and justify your planned course of action.

> What is "proof of concept"? It can take years to get the data you'll need to prove something really works. Build off of pilots or ideas that have already been validated to show that your solution is feasible, and you have the rationale for why it should work.

What'd you find?

Activity #3: Explore Blogs and Books and Apps

Many great teacher-driven models already exist and are waiting for you to apply them to your situation. Again, it will be *yours* because you'll put your spin on any ideas you find.

We LOVE:

Blogs: Edutopia and Cult of Pedagogy

Books that "get" the world of teaching: Times 10 Publications and others

Apps: Nearpod, Explain Everything, Mural, Trello

What'd you find?

Activity #4: Tap Into Your PLN

Ask! Ask your colleagues, ask on social media, ask a teacher at another school. Just ask. Maybe people will point you toward apps or tools that will take your solution to the next level. Meanwhile, you'll be building relationships and honoring the expertise of other educators. Win-win!

> When can you learn from others? Over lunch, over coffee, during team meetings, during staff meetings, through email, via text, on social media, over the phone, passing a note, or popping your head in the door.

What'd you find?

Activities to Tap Into User Input

Think about it. It happens to us all the time as teachers: We get asked for our input, but that input either gets discarded or the idea is implemented in such a ridiculous way it makes us want to pull out our hair. This section is here so we don't do that to our users. You already talked with your users when you were developing a solution, and now it's time to take that a step further and get their input on the best way to implement that solution.

Use this box to get the voice and validation you need from your users to ensure your idea is successful. If your users don't like your idea or how you've implemented it, you're in for an uphill battle. It's much more effective to ask than to assume, so here are strategies to empathize with your user.

Activity #1: Yin and Yang Exercise: Capturing Opposites

It can be easier to express the negatives about a situation than the positives. For instance, over the years we've tried numerous times to ask our students what they were passionate about—and were usually met with blank looks. Fortunately, we discovered when we flipped it to a negative, it was often easier for students to express themselves. Therefore, when we asked them what issues made them angry, they came alive (and we uncovered that passion!). When seeking input, frame your question as a positive and then as a negative. There's no shame in using different strategies to get people to open up.

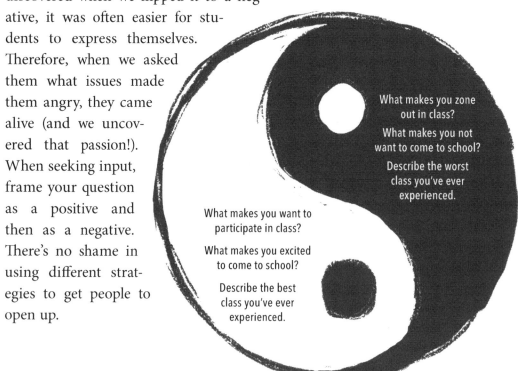

What makes you zone out in class?

What makes you not want to come to school?

Describe the worst class you've ever experienced.

What makes you want to participate in class?

What makes you excited to come to school?

Describe the best class you've ever experienced.

Activity #2: Start, Stop, Continue

With students, make a simple list of things they would like to start doing, stop doing, and continue doing. This simple activity can be done individually or as a whole group: make a big "start, stop, continue" chart (in your room or virtually using an app like Padlet or a shared document), give students Post-its (real or virtual), and have them add to each column. Debrief as a whole class and add any additional ideas.

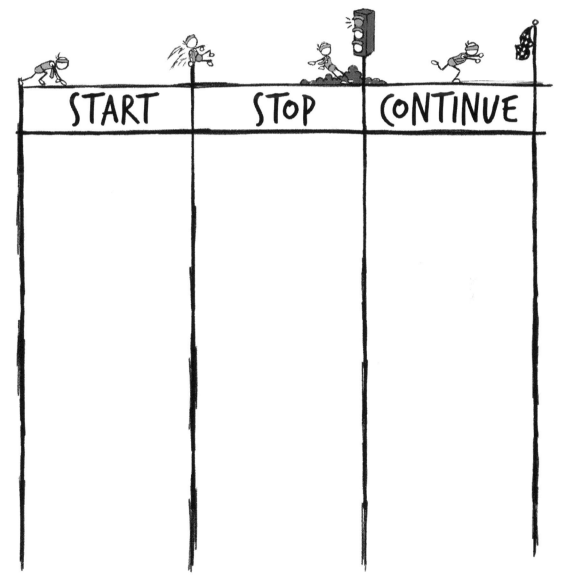

Activity #3: Direct Feedback

Create a flyer for this project and pitch it to your students. Are they in? Do they like it? Have them grade you—either with a survey, exit ticket, or rubric. Check your scores and revise from there. (It's also a great way to test out and revise a rubric.)

Activity #4: Recognizing Informal Feedback

Keep a notepad handy to jot down indirect feedback. These are the questions, complaints, and confusion that arise when your user is taking part in your idea or project. Capture this informal feedback and realize that your user is indirectly telling you what you need to do to improve.

Activity #5: Onboarding Activity

Who wants to join the design team for this project? Assemble a small committee, council of advisors, or team of students to provide a perspective you don't have. Make it a real position; have a clear title, clear expectations, and compensation (volunteer hours, snacks).

Remember: Kids have talents we don't have, including tech know-how, artistic abilities, and creative thinking. Trust us: You want them on your team.

As you're implementing an idea, take notes when people ask questions, get confused, or voice complaints. Don't take these comments personally; this is how people communicate that something is unclear, and it provides valuable feedback as to how we can improve a project.

Get Organized: Deep Dives to Outline Your Logistics

Summary

Ever noticed it's the little things that trip up a project? At our workshops, people often tell us what they're going to do without thinking what those actions actually entail. They tend to leave the details up in the air, causing projects to flop. Groups frequently think they're on the same page, but when each group member starts listing details, it becomes evident that each person has a different vision for how the work will unfold.

This section is all about getting into the nitty-gritty of project planning: Clearly defining what your solution and implementation look like, securing your supplies, getting organized, knowing where to go, ensuring you have the right players at the table, and assigning clear to-dos. By thoroughly completing the boxes in this section, you'll create accountability and determine who and what you need to succeed.

Use activities in this section to:

- Ensure everyone's on the same page and understands exactly what needs to be done to complete the project.

- Assign roles and responsibilities to maximize your team's talents.

- Create accountability for you, for others, and for everyone.

- Think through needed resources.

Tasks

- What tangible things do you need to produce for this to happen?
- What are your concrete next steps and who is accountable for each?
- Which tasks could you pass on to others outside your team?

Resources

- What key inputs do you need to complete your task?
  - Space • Tools • Funding • Expertise

Partners

- How will you engage needed stakeholders with the project?
- How will you pitch your idea to others?
- Who would enhance this project?

LOGISTICS

Activities to Articulate Tasks

Okay, let's be real here. Sometimes we have a clear vision of what we want to accomplish but struggle to break the solution into manageable steps and tasks. Use these activities to define the tangible steps to make this project happen. Don't assume everyone can or will get everything done. Providing concrete details and hammering out your logistics will lead you to success.

Activity #1: List and Assign

Write down what needs to be done/produced to make your idea happen.

- Divide and conquer in a way that fits your project and team.

- Determine who's best suited to complete which task(s).

- Determine how autonomous each person/task will be.

Activity #2: Question and Clarify

 Once tasks are broken down and assigned, question everything. What does that mean? People often tell us things like: "I'm going to round up volunteers." Or "I'm going to create a toolkit." And we always ask, "What does that mean?" What does that look like in action? Is that an email, a flyer, attending a networking event, making an announcement at the PTA meeting? Is it done virtually or on paper, how are you packaging it, how do people access and learn about it? So ... question and clarify.

Have each person write, draw out, or talk through what they are doing. As you share, look for overlaps, duplication, and areas that are still too big.

Then ask yourselves the "Are you all on the same page?" questions in the note below.

Keep revising and adding details until everyone and everything is clear.

Are you all on the same page?

☐ Does everyone fully understand the scope and parameters of their task(s)?

☐ Do you understand what you've been asked to do and how to do it?

☐ Do you understand *how* each person is going to do what they say they are going to do? Do you know *when*? Do tasks have clear timelines, particularly those tasks that depend on other tasks?

☐ What do we need to further break down? Look for overlaps, duplication, and areas that are still too big.

Activity #3: KISS: Keep It Simple, Stupid

Ask yourself:

1. Are these the vital, necessary steps you need to accomplish your goal?

2. Can you cut out anything?

3. Can you simplify anything that's gotten overly complicated?

Activities to Explore Resources

What do you need to accomplish this project, to complete your tasks? These activities are about how to be resourceful to get what you need, find resources that already exist, and consider what you ideally want.

Activity #1: Articulating Needs Versus Wants

As we've said before, the more specific you can be, the more you can visualize and articulate *exactly* what you are doing, the greater the likelihood for success. So be specific in what you need in order to get this work done. We also encourage you to list your wants to help paint a clearer vision of your ideal. Use this chart to brainstorm what you *need* and dream about what you might *want* for your project.

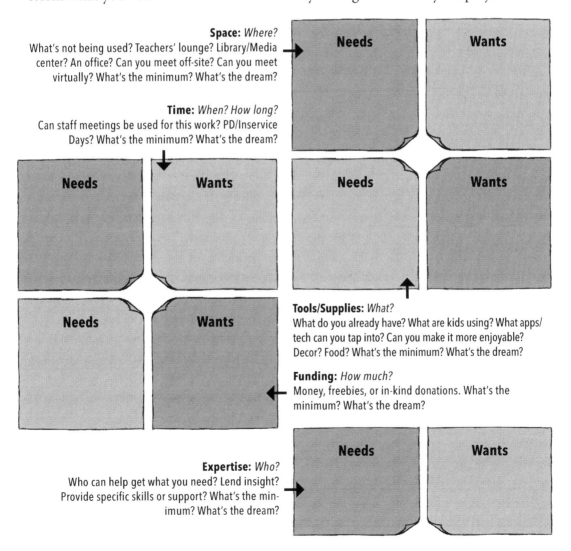

Space: *Where?*
What's not being used? Teachers' lounge? Library/Media center? An office? Can you meet off-site? Can you meet virtually? What's the minimum? What's the dream?

Time: *When? How long?*
Can staff meetings be used for this work? PD/Inservice Days? What's the minimum? What's the dream?

Tools/Supplies: *What?*
What do you already have? What are kids using? What apps/tech can you tap into? Can you make it more enjoyable? Decor? Food? What's the minimum? What's the dream?

Funding: *How much?*
Money, freebies, or in-kind donations. What's the minimum? What's the dream?

Expertise: *Who?*
Who can help get what you need? Lend insight? Provide specific skills or support? What's the minimum? What's the dream?

Needs | Wants (repeated for each category)

Activities to Nurture Partnerships

We often talk about building community but don't have the opportunity to brainstorm how we can make those connections. It's easy to focus on a "team" (those directly working with you on a project, often from/in your building) and stop there. But a whole world is out there that we need to keep in mind. Use the following activities and consider people and groups you could partner with to help propel, enhance, or complete your project.

Partners are *not* your core group/team. Strategic partners can help you take your project to the next level.

Activity 1: Get the Green Light

Who (if anyone) do you need support from so you can get a green light and move forward with this idea? Brainstorm who exactly you might need permission from as well as those you may need to keep in the loop.

Activity #2: Cultivate Potential Partnership Opportunities

Partnerships in education are about joining forces and thinking outside the box on who can enhance your project. For example: Say you want to revamp an unused part of the schoolyard and turn it into a garden. You're tight on resources, but need to get the garden in better shape. You learn that a Girl Scout troop holds their meetings at the school. You talk with the troop leader and find out the girls are trying to earn a certain badge, and cleaning up the yard would be a perfect way to do that.

What partnership potential exists with:

- Colleagues: Teachers, staff, custodians, admin … consider everyone. (You won't believe the resources a custodian can help you find.)
- Parents, grandparents, guardians: They are education stakeholders. Involve them.
- Students: They know and can do more than we think. Empower them.
- After-school programs, clubs, activities: Many groups are looking for service projects or ways to help support the community. Find a connection.
- Libraries, community centers, retirement homes: Between their staff, participants, and residents, they hold a wealth of experience and know-how, waiting to be tapped.
- Nonprofits, businesses: Beyond just asking for financial support, explore how they can help you build up and implement your project. They are experts: use them!

Activity #3: Pitch It

You've identified people to enhance your project, but how will you pitch your idea so others engage in it? Be intentional. As a general rule, your message/delivery should include the following three elements:

- What are you doing and how does it add value?
- How would they benefit from this idea/project?
- What's your call to action for them? (What exactly would you like them to do?)

Then, keep your *user* (who you are asking, in this case) in mind and contact them in the most appropriate and appealing way, be it a phone call, email, social media message, or personal visit. Finally, consider who should make the request. Kids are powerful allies when asking for help.

Our Pitch For: _____

- Contact method:
- Who will contact:
- What are you doing and how does it add value?
- How would they benefit from this idea/project?
- What's your call to action for them?

Our Pitch For: _____

- Contact method:
- Who will contact:
- What are you doing and how does it add value?
- How would they benefit from this idea/project?
- What's your call to action for them?

Be Prepared: Deep Dives to Maximize Your Execution

Summary:

Innovating in education can leave us feeling like we're being pulled in ten different directions. Let's get tactical and focus on how to execute ideas and anticipate setbacks. Building from the boxes in the logistics section, the execution column will help you think strategically about tasks, resources, and partners so you can realistically get things done.

Remember: Innovating and problem-solving equal change. Change can often cause stress. Use this section to help minimize setbacks and drama by anticipating roadblocks and mitigating unnecessary tension.

Use activities in this section to:

- Anticipate roadblocks so you can adapt more nimbly and continue moving forward.

- Ditch drama so you'll be free to focus on what really matters: creating the best implementation for students.

- Pace your project to avoid feeling overwhelmed.

Timeline

- Which tasks have the highest priority?
- When does each task need to be completed by?

Strategy

- How are you going to obtain your resources?
- List three things that might go wrong with your plan and how you will overcome.

Managing Relationships

- What's each team member's role and how will you communicate?
- Can you set up a designated spot and time to work?
- How might your solution impact others and how might you manage change or stress?

EXECUTION

Activities to Establish a Timeline

Timing is everything. Avoid stress by pacing your project so it doesn't become a burden. Don't bite off more than you can chew; make this experience as low-stress as possible by setting realistic short- and long-term deadlines.

> The problems in education aren't going anywhere; it's okay to take your time, preserve your sanity, and avoid burnout.

Activity #1: Time Management

Avoid adding more to your plate. Think through your daily routine.

Where/when can you make time for this work?

Are there tasks that someone else can do? Who?

Are there any tasks you can get rid of?

Activity #2: Deadlines

Look back at your task sheet and assign deadlines for key tasks for further account-ability. Be realistic with these! If you have a lot going on, give yourself extra time.

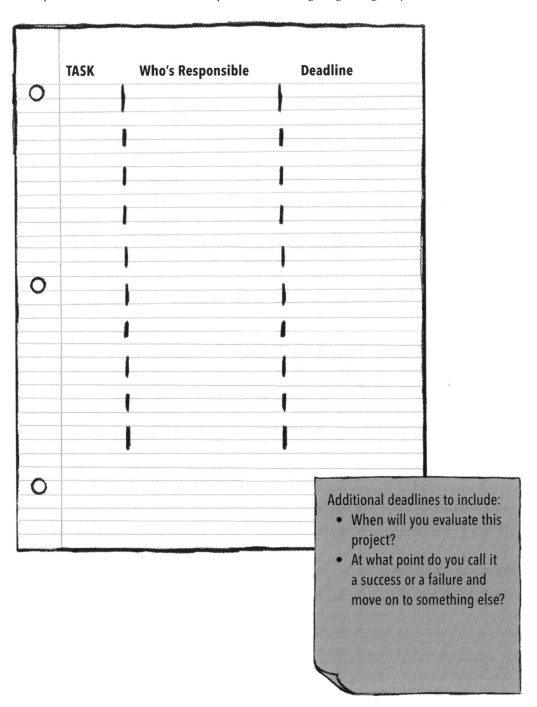

TASK	Who's Responsible	Deadline

Additional deadlines to include:
- When will you evaluate this project?
- At what point do you call it a success or a failure and move on to something else?

Activities to Build a Strategy

When you started this project, you probably had a few roadblocks in mind that might stymie the work, such as a lack of funding, time, or space, or *that* colleague who just poo-poos everything. This section is designed to give you a mental game plan on how to push through those common obstacles that slow or stop projects. See Module Five for more tips and ideas.

Activity #1: Obtaining Resources: The Great Asking Game

Listing materials, spaces, and expertise is the easy part; how to obtain those resources is where it gets tricky. Use this space to figure out who you need to ask or what you need to do to obtain the resources essential to your project. This game requires you to—wait for it—ask people. Don't let the fear of a no stop you from asking! It's always amazing what random items neighbors, family members, students, and the community have that can be put to good use.

If you don't ask, no one can help you. The worst that someone can say is no. And you'll be amazed at what people are willing to do when you ask.

When making a request, be:
- Specific in your request
- Specific about how it benefits students
- Specific with your thanks

Who can help get what you need? Lend insight? Provide specific skills or support? Look to:

- Your principal/administration
- Individuals/friends
- Chamber of Commerce
- Local service organizations
- Virtual connections: find experts and ask them for a fifteen-minute Q&A
- Social media: you'll be amazing at who will answer a few quick questions when asked

Activity #2: The Roadblocks

You probably already have an idea of what might stand in your way, slow you down, or limit your project. Instead of stressing, get proactive.

Examples:

- You know Wi-Fi isn't going to work every day. What's your backup plan?

- You know you need to raise money. How will you execute your fundraising plan?

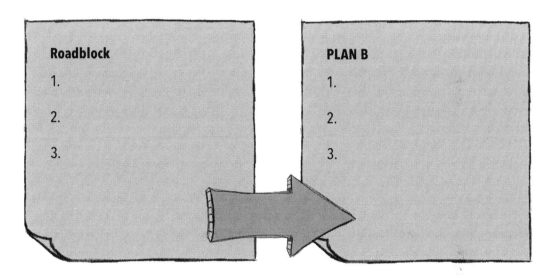

Roadblock

1.

2.

3.

PLAN B

1.

2.

3.

Activities to Manage Relationships

As we've emphasized, education is an industry built on relationships. We want you to innovate with as little drama as possible. This section will help you think through the people who will be involved and outline how to create and maintain a positive atmosphere while overcoming setbacks.

Activity #1: Keep Group Dynamics Good–Managing Your Team Relationships

Foster open and honest communication by setting expectations. Getting (and keeping) everyone on the same page as you work through the project will minimize unnecessary stress.

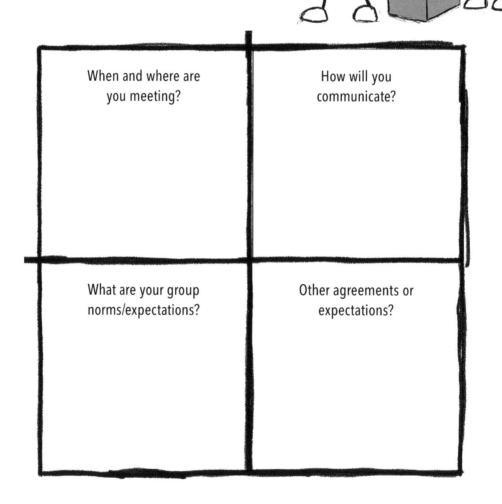

When and where are you meeting?	How will you communicate?
What are your group norms/expectations?	Other agreements or expectations?

Activity #2: Keep Resistance Low–Help Manage Change

It sounds odd, but your project may impact others in your building who aren't part of the project. Be transparent about what you are doing and why, and you will help minimize hurt feelings and unnecessary resistance.

> Who needs to know about this project?

> Who outside your building might object to your work?

> How can you communicate and mitigate objections?

> Who needs to at least be in the loop?

> Who will be the loudest critic? Why? How could you ease their mind?

Activity #3: Ditch Drama by Keeping the Peace

If you're expecting resistance from your students (or other users), this may be about building and nurturing relationships. Head on over to Module Three for strategies to flex your leadership skills.

Final Thoughts

"Words may show a man's wit, but actions his meaning."
—Benjamin Franklin
"The most effective way to do it is to do it."
— Amelia Earhart

Congratulations, you've made it through your first Canvas!

All action starts with an idea, a dream of what we hope to accomplish. Perhaps it's that perfect vision we have at the start of each new school year of what our classroom will look and feel like, how we will captivate and inspire every day, and Mary Poppins-like lead our students to great new heights of learning.

> Get *credit* for your problem-solving work. See Module Five for more information about using the Canvas for PD credit.

Dreaming is easy (and a wonderful source of inspiration), but innovating—acting—is hard. And *you* did it. While many people will only see the end product of your idea, we know the hours and hours of trial and error and careful planning that went into the process. Like the lessons, projects, and other initiatives you've created for your students, we want to thank you for putting your blood, sweat, and tears into this work and commend you on a job well done.

We know implementation is everything. Given the daily grind of teaching—the planning and prepping, the revolving and expanding demands, the lack of strategic problem-solving training and support—it's no wonder teachers' great ideas frequently end up on the back burner, waiting for the time, resources, space, or leadership to take shape. Kudos to you for taking this step to create the classroom you crave and that students deserve. You are the best problem-solver in education. You know your students, what they need, and how to help them reach their full potential.

> Sometimes all you need is a helping hand, a little push, or maybe a kick in the pants. Let the Canvas be your kick.

We don't have the answers to all the woes of education, but collectively, teachers do. We hope you can continue to use this tool to get those conversations going and make more ideas a reality.

Reflections, Ideas, and Notes

Module Three:

Startup Your Leadership Skills:

Strategies to Build Relationships and Engage Others in Your Work

In this module:

- Leadership: The neglected aspect of innovation
- Tap into your leadership potential
- Transformational leadership in a nutshell
- The principles of transformational leadership: Activities to grow your leadership skills

  - ▶ Individualized consideration: Meeting people where they're at
  - ▶ Inspirational motivation: Engage others to be a part of your work
  - ▶ Intellectual stimulation: Tap into the talent that surrounds you
  - ▶ Idealized influence: Be the change you want to see

- Final thoughts

Leadership: The Neglected Aspect of Innovation

leader noun

lead er | \ ˈlē-dər \

Definition of *leader*

1 : something that leads: such as

2 : a person who has commanding authority or influence

You may have asked yourself why we would pick leadership as a key module of *The Startup Teacher Playbook*. We had a clear reason: we've seen a lot of projects fall flat because people couldn't work together.

As many of you have likely experienced, new ideas, new projects, change, and innovation can come with a lot of emotion and a bit of drama—basically, stress. The Canvas allows you to work on the more tangible parts of project planning, but now it's time to focus on how we deal with all of those intangible factors (people) that will ultimately make or break your project.

Hence this section about leadership. Developing your leadership skills will help you exercise your soft skills so you can recognize others' needs and navigate accordingly. It will enhance your ability to work well with others, to get buy-in on your ideas, and to motivate others to work *with you*. When you learn about leadership and build your leadership capacity, you're developing strategies that will strengthen your EQ (emotional intelligence) so you can effectively build relationships. In turn, you will be able to *strategically* think about how you interact with others so you can help them reach their greatest potential, and you can reach yours.

Developing your leadership capacity will not only help you materialize your Educator Canvas, it will help you be a better teacher. Period. Even if you aren't working on a project right now, we are absolutely positive you will find useful aspects of this module that apply to your work as an educator.

This section will help you *(note how the skills build on each other):*

 1. **Recognize leadership opportunities on any given day.** Whether formal (leading your class, training adults, spearheading a project) or informal (sitting in meetings, interactions in the lounge and hallways), you are always working with people. Take advantage of every opportunity to get closer to your objectives.

 2. **Develop your soft skills and increase your emotional intelligence.** When you take time to build your emotional intelligence, you gain strategies to navigate and motivate others.

 3. **Increase your teaching power.** By focusing on motivating others, you'll also gain skills at ditching drama and elevating student voice, both of which should increase performance and joy.

 4. **Model what good leadership looks like.** Whether it's for your students, for your colleagues, or for the general public, when you build your soft skills and model what good leadership looks like— really allow others to *see* what leadership can be—you, in turn, help them develop their leadership capacity.

 5. **Increase project productivity and success and amplify your impact.** By developing your leadership capacity and enhancing your emotional intelligence, you're better equipped to lead others. This will increase productivity and get your ideas off the ground more effectively.

Tap Into Your Leadership Potential

We recognize you're leading your classroom, perhaps the project you've designed with the Educator Canvas, but you have the chance to act as a leader through nearly *every* interaction you have. As educators, we constantly encounter leadership opportunities, but don't always recognize them, let alone take advantage of them.

Through our workshops, we've been able to highlight the five most common missed leadership opportunities among educators, opportunities that hold our ideas and our projects back. We mention them because they demonstrate the power *you* have to control situations, and that tapping into your leadership potential is key to innovating in education.

Missed Opportunity #1:
Talking with administration or other decision-makers.

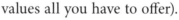

We've encountered a surprising number of teachers who will not move forward with an idea if they have to reach out to their principal or an administrator. They are reluctant to express their viewpoints or feelings, to set up a meeting, or even send an email. If you find that you're intimidated by your administration, it's time to tap into your leadership potential (or, unfortunately in some cases, find a school that values all you have to offer).

Missed Opportunity #2:
Working with colleagues.

Many teachers resist working with their colleagues. Teaching can be an oddly isolating profession, and it can be hard to exit the little island you've built for yourself. We understand that flying solo can feel easier, less complicated, oddly peaceful, and even safer than interacting with other adults in the building. We get that. But sequestering yourself on your island will only take you so far. Staying isolated and limiting your connections will ultimately cap your potential to impact student learning. If this sounds like you, use the activities in this section and take steps, however small, to get off your island.

Missed Opportunity #3:
Working with your students.

We often ask teachers: Are you managing your class-room or are you leading it? Leading it means actively seeking out student voice and choice. You create the sensation that you are going through the learning process *together*. You encourage students to achieve their highest potential. It's obvious that you value students' needs, opinions, and feelings through the teaching and learning that take place in your classroom. You set a high bar, and students understand the vision/mission of your class and work with you to achieve it. Ask yourself: Would my students agree that I'm achieving this? If not, tap into your leadership potential to make that change.

Missed Opportunity #4:
Working with parents or the wider community.

Do you tap into all the potential resources and allies that might be at your fingertips? Sometimes we miss out on making connections, creating synergies, and finding opportunities we might not have known existed. Potential and invaluable partners are all around you. Leadership helps you to reach out and make connections, including to parents, local organizations, or other entities. So many connections can help us achieve a greater impact.

Are you boosting and enhancing performance fully and to the maximum potential?

Do you tap into:

- Colleagues with years of experience
- Colleagues fresh out of school or new to your school
- Colleagues in different grades
- Colleagues in different disciplines
- Administration and district staff
- Secretaries
- Support staff
- Custodians
- Students
- Social media
- Experts (via books, conferences, and articles)
- Parents/guardians/grandparents
- Community and business leaders

Missed Opportunity #5: Navigating around toxicity.

We've seen it countless times: A teacher (or team) sucks in their breath at the thought of that *one* person who they know will hold back their project. Let's face it: Our colleagues can be more challenging than the students. While you do *not* have to like everyone you work with, leading does require strategy and empathy so you can work with all sorts of personalities. If you find yourself being drained by a specific individual, tap into leadership to re-energize and strategize around that person. One person should not have the power to disrupt your ideas or projects.

Developing our leadership skills helps us build our emotional intelligence, recognize others' needs, and navigate accordingly. Instead of letting others drain you, consider what's at the heart of their behavior and how to work around it:

The Busy Body. Their nose is in everything and they spread gossip faster than a cold in an elementary school. Consider: Is that person lonely and looking to make connections?

The Burnout. They've seen it all and done it all and have no interest in trying something "new" because they already tried it (and it didn't work), and next year there will be something new, so why bother? Consider: Has that person been hurt by years of rejection? Has the profession killed their enthusiasm?

The Miserable A-hole. Negativity oozes out of them and infects anyone who comes near. Nothing is good enough, nothing will work, nothing is worth trying. Consider: Is that person lashing out because they aren't happy with themselves or life? Might they be suffering from years of hearing negative responses to their ideas?

The Emotionally Unstable Mess. They are overwhelmed by life, and any new task or request is enough to make them crack. They might put on a brave face, but their stress is palpable. Consider: Has that person gone through a personal issue or rough patch and gotten to the point where they can't handle any more stress?

Transformational Leadership in a Nutshell

The type of leader you have, the type of leader you are, matters. A lot. Different styles of leadership generate different results and different experiences. As a learning designer, how you run your classroom, how you work with others, will determine the degree to which you are successful, especially when it comes to getting big ideas off the ground. All educators should naturally be trained to be the type of leader that brings joy, engagement, satisfaction, and productivity to students.

Unfortunately, teachers are not trained to be leaders. We think that's because there's a bit of an archaic view of what leadership is in the education space. For one, leadership is often synonymous with administration. This neglectful use of the word shuts down conversation and creates an unnecessary hierarchy of power. To help teachers harness their power to make change, we began to wonder how we could train teachers to think differently about leadership.

Looking up leadership courses in education often led us to certificates and modules on how to move up the career ladder: a dead end. We knew that developing leadership skills were critical to helping teachers innovate, but even after we made this discovery, we were struggling to find ways to actually *do* that.

Business leaders seek leadership training with an eye toward higher profits: How can I boost my team's performance to boost productivity to increase profits?

We have a much greater goal:
How can I increase the productivity and skill of my team (students or colleagues or whomever you're working with) to increase outcomes for students?

Doing what we do best, we decided to seek inspiration from the business world by exploring how the most inspirational business leaders developed their skills to work with their employees, help them reach their highest potential, and make things happen (which is essentially what we do as teachers).

That's when we discovered Transformational Leadership, a highly talked about and researched form of leadership that provides practical strategies to heighten our emotional intelligence and inform how we guide others. In education, we often talk about emotional intelligence, but aren't always given strategies to develop it with others. After attending a certificate program on innovative leadership (at a leading business school), the dots connected and we realized that we had found our path forward with Transformational Leadership. We just needed to adapt what we had learned and apply it to the education space. Et voila! This module.

For us, transformational leadership is like project management on steroids. It goes way beyond day-to-day organization and planning and taps into the human element of project planning that is so often ignored. It will help you think strategically about your interactions, tapping into strategies that will help you build and nurture relationships, manage emotions, reduce drama, and navigate difficult situations so you ultimately have greater success with any challenge, change, or project.

For all you nerds out there who need the formal definition (don't worry, we fall into the category), here's our favorite: "Transformational leadership is defined as a leadership approach that causes change in individuals and social systems. In its ideal form, it creates valuable and positive change in the followers with the end goal of developing followers into leaders. Enacted in its authentic form, transformational leadership enhances the motivation, morale, and performance of followers through a variety of mechanisms. These include connecting the follower's sense of identity and self to the mission and the collective identity of the organization; being a role model for followers that inspires them; challenging followers to take greater ownership for their work; and understanding the strengths and weaknesses of followers so the leader can align followers with tasks that optimize their performance ..." (Transformational Leadership, Langston EDU).

The Principles of Transformational Leadership: Activities to Grow Your Leadership Skills

No matter how you see yourself, no matter what you think your strengths are, leadership is a skill *anyone* can nurture and improve. It's not about having a certain personality. There's not necessarily a "leadership type." As with learning any skill, it's a matter of deciding you want to improve how you work with others, then systematically developing the soft skills that will heighten your emotional intelligence. Use these strategies to help you do that.

Transformational leadership is defined by four major elements, all of which connect to the classroom and our work as educators. In the following pages, we'll break down each element further, but here's the nutshell version (yes, there is overlap here):

Individualized Consideration: This section is about understanding the needs and interests of others. It's about recognizing what motivates and drives people and gaining their perspective on issues. It's about tapping into their heart, curiosity, and abilities, and applying those to your work. Go to page 144.

Inspirational Motivation: Learn how to articulate your vision clearly so others *want* to engage in your process, especially when life is pulling them in many different directions. Practice effective communication and differentiate how you can best support your followers. Go to page 159.

Intellectual Stimulation: This section will help you spark curiosity in others and help them to realize their full potential. It will encourage you to assume the best in people and trust them to find solutions to challenges you've presented. Go to page 172.

Idealized Influence: Use these strategies to model your ethics and values. Ensure you're walking the talk in all you say and do. Go to page 182.

This box provides guiding questions to help you gauge which leadership areas are most relevant to you and your work:

Individualized Consideration:
- Are you gathering other people's perspectives? Are you listening and understanding where they're coming from?
- Are you meeting people where they're at?
- Do you understand their goals and what motivates them?

Intellectual Stimulation:
- Are you able to engage others to do something about a problem?
- Do you provide space and opportunities for others to collaborate, explore new ideas, and think creatively?
- Do you show you trust and support others to take ownership over their ideas?

Inspirational Motivation:
Do you have a clear vision and aligned goals for what you want to achieve?
- Do you know how to get others to care about your vision or goals?
- Are you able to sell your idea and get buy-in from the people you're trying to engage?
- Do you set high, yet achievable, standards for others to follow?

Idealized Influence:
- Do you walk the talk and show people commitment and dedication to projects?
- Do you practice what you preach by role-modeling your values and ethics?
- Do you manage emotions and minimize drama?

After working with hundreds of teachers on countless project ideas, we know how important it is for teachers to see themselves as leaders and harness their leadership skills to instigate change. We want you to have the greatest impact possible, so play your way through this section and gain greater insights and skills to lead the change you wish to see.

As with the other parts of this book, you do *not* have to read this straight through! As you peruse the sections of this module, you will naturally gravitate toward the topics that apply to you and the issues you're dealing with. Take what you need and skip what you don't. Regardless of which strategies and activities you decide to employ, you will gain greater insights and skills into your role as a leader. We invite you to come back time and again to uncover new ways to grow as a leader so you can best materialize the change you wish to see.

About these activities:

- You may see some overlap in the elements of transformational leadership. We did our best to translate it to the education space.

- The activities are meant to get you thinking; they are a starting place, not a final destination.

- Use this with your colleagues and students (or anyone else).

- This section is all about building up these soft skills so you can become a better leader. Some examples apply to the classroom and some to working with your peers; take and adapt accordingly.

Individualized Consideration: Meeting People Where They're At

 Checklist: Boosting Individualized Consideration
Take a moment to reflect on the following leadership strategies and see if any apply to your work.

I want to uncover more ways to:

- Tune in to others. Go to page 145.

- Ask, listen, and understand. Go to page 147.

- Provide outlets to engage others in self-discovery and strength-finding. Go to page 149.

- Encourage people to choose, adapt, or personalize work that nurtures their strengths and interests. Go to page 151.

- Provide ways to support individuals to work through tasks or goals. Go to page 152.

- Recognize and give praise to others in a way that is meaningful. Go to page 154.

- Manage expectations and stress. Go to page 157.

> This section is all about paying attention to those around you. It's about listening to others, seeing others, and feeling with and for others in order to know their perspectives, motivations, and goals. Doing so will help you gain the insights you need to engage others in your work. It will help you to make connections with others so those you're working with feel that you hear their voices and value them.

Tuning In to Others

It can be easy to get caught in our own bubbles; to forget a world is out there beyond our own. It happens to us all. If we want to be better leaders, the first step is to open our eyes and ears. When we think beyond our own needs and stay open, we remember there are multiple ways to do things and so much that others have to offer.

Activity #1: The Perfect Gift: Tuning In to People's Wants and Desires

Take a moment to reflect. Think about the people closest to you right now. It could be anyone: your family, your students, your colleagues, your friends, your neighbors, your spouse. How are they? Think deeply: Have you taken time to check in? Make sure everyone's genuinely well? Do you know what's happening in their lives? What they're excited about? What's stressing them out? If not, take a moment to check in and reconnect.

Imagine you have to give a perfect gift (and we don't necessarily mean items you buy at the store) to each of the closest people in your life. What pops into your mind?

Neighbor

Colleague

Significant Other

Parent

Child

Friend

If you get the opportunity, *ask* them what they would consider the "perfect gift." Remember, we're not just talking about materialistic things. Compare their answers with yours. Were you able to tap into their wants and desires?

Activity #2: Appreciate That There's More Than One Way to Do Something

Grab a partner (in person or virtually). Imagine that you're each headed to the beach. Separately, write a list of what you would pack for your day of fun in the sun.

When you're finished, compare and reflect. How similar were your lists? Where did you agree? What did they pack that you completely forgot? If you have time, ask a third and fourth person to make a list, too, and see how their lists differ.

> The point? There is more than one way to do something. Stay open to other people's processes and ideas as you embark on projects together. By listening to others and tapping into their perspectives, you'll have a much better outcome.

Create Opportunities to Ask, Listen, and Understand

This section is about creating opportunities to connect with those around you. Use these activities to grow relationships and have more meaningful conversations.

Activity #1: Dip Your Toes: Small Ways to Start Conversations

Say hello!
It's easy to get so caught up in our day that we forget to say hi in the hallway, greet our students, or check in with a colleague. These greetings are simple enough, but easy to let fall to the wayside.

I will greet:

Maximize lunch.
It can be great to have a productive lunch, or just use that time to unwind. It's also a perfect time to build relationships. Take time to sit with your students or colleagues for lunch and connect about topics other than school. Notice someone who doesn't go to lunch? Seek them out and connect.

I will eat with:

Activity #2: Wade In: Creating Time and Space for Deeper Conversations

Exit tickets.
Create a daily strategy for getting student input.

My exit ticket plan:

Connection questions.
Give students opportunities to share what's on their mind and happening in their lives. Try asking the question, "I wish my teacher/colleague knew ..." or inviting them to share moments of joy. What else have you wanted to try?

Connection to-dos:

Make yourself available.
Find or create an outlet that allows people to reach out to you in a way they're comfortable with. Ideas?

My where and when:

Activity #3: Hit the Deep End: Fully Immerse Yourself in Dialogue

Conversation menus.
Deep conversations help others build connections. Use a conversation menu to help people achieve a higher-level discussion than usual.

I will use this:

Fishbowl.
Great for groups of fifteen to thirty. Encourage people to share their points of view and opinions on an open-ended topic. You'll gain keen insights you might not otherwise be able to uncover.

I will use this:

Gum ball discussion.
A fun, interactive way to gather responses visually and creatively to a series of questions.

I will use this:

Instructions for these activities (and many more) can be found in the resources section in Module Five.

Empathy is the ability to understand and share another's feelings. It's an incredibly powerful tool for any leader. Check out courses on Human-Centered Design or Implicit Bias if you wish to grow this skill.

Provide Outlets to Engage Others in Self-Discovery and Strengths Finding

This section is all about helping others uncover more about themselves and what they bring to the table. The more you cultivate the talents of others, the more benefits your team will reap. When others know their passions and strengths, it's easier for them to see how they add value to a project. Once they know that, they'll start to feel like an integral part of the team.

Activity #1: Offer a Strengths-Finding Consultation

Set aside one-on-one time to have a deep conversation and help an individual uncover their strengths. During the conversation, ask them to reflect on their experiences and tell you what strengths they think they possess. Give them the opportunity to explore and recognize what you've noticed as well.

Prep yourself before the meeting:
What comes naturally to this person?
What sets them apart?
When do they seem to shine?

NOTE: This is not about labeling anyone. It's about helping people see their talents and abilities and nurturing them.

Activity #2: Run a Mini-360

Have students write their name on a piece of paper. Pass the papers around and ask everyone else to write the adjective that comes to mind when they think of that person. What traits appear? Were they surprising? How can you ensure you're working in a way that utilizes those qualities?

Activity #3: Help Others Focus on What Energizes Them

Fortunately, we don't need to be good at everything. Use this activity to gain insights on strengths and weaknesses.

Strengths aren't just what people are good at. They are what give people energy. It's easier for people to develop that area because they enjoy doing it.

When working on something, I feel joy/ energized when (e.g., I work alone; I work in a team; conducting research; developing a presentation):

When working on a project, I feel drained when:

Weaknesses aren't necessarily what they aren't good at, but activities that drain their energy. It's hard to improve because working on those areas is exhausting.

Activities like these are sometimes incorrectly used to determine whether you're a leader. That's not the point. Uncover how you like to work and what synergies you have as a team.

Activity #4: Host a Good Old Team-Builder

Head over to Google and find a team-builder activity that *your* team might enjoy. We know team-building activities can cause groans, but if you pick the right one, they can offer insights into your team dynamics. After, make sure to take time to reflect: Which parts did people enjoy? Which parts were stressful or exhausting? (It usually varies for everyone.)

Encourage People to Choose, Adapt, or Personalize Work That Nurtures Their Strengths and Interests

These exercises are all about allowing others to take ownership over an idea or project so they can personalize their learning and work. Use these activities to divvy up project tasks and assign roles—with students, colleagues, or the community—more efficiently and effectively.

Activity #1: Be Intentional About Providing Choice

Where are the opportunities for people to personalize their work? How can you maintain your vision while allowing space for others to run with their ideas?

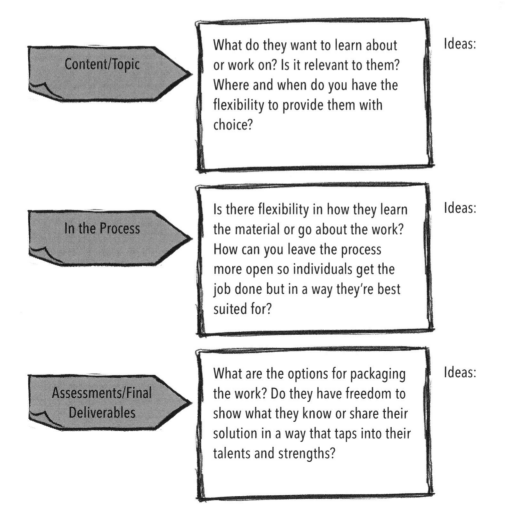

Content/Topic

What do they want to learn about or work on? Is it relevant to them? Where and when do you have the flexibility to provide them with choice?

Ideas:

In the Process

Is there flexibility in how they learn the material or go about the work? How can you leave the process more open so individuals get the job done but in a way they're best suited for?

Ideas:

Assessments/Final Deliverables

What are the options for packaging the work? Do they have freedom to show what they know or share their solution in a way that taps into their talents and strengths?

Ideas:

Provide Support Structures and Feedback Loops

These activities are all about helping you to be the best coach and mentor you can be. Making yourself accessible and learning to give (and receive) feedback will help you show others how to take their work to a new level.

Activity #1: Reflection: Are You Accessible?

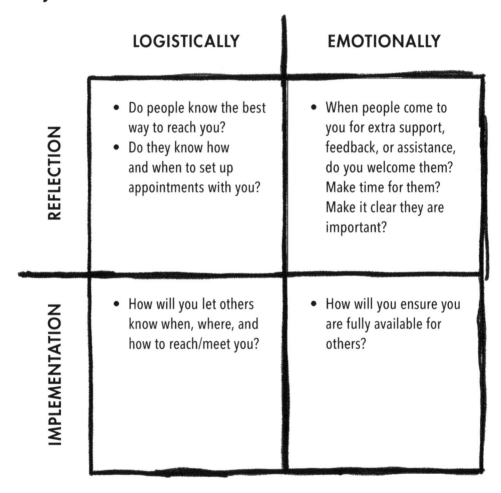

LOGISTICALLY

EMOTIONALLY

REFLECTION

- Do people know the best way to reach you?
- Do they know how and when to set up appointments with you?

- When people come to you for extra support, feedback, or assistance, do you welcome them? Make time for them? Make it clear they are important?

IMPLEMENTATION

- How will you let others know when, where, and how to reach/meet you?

- How will you ensure you are fully available for others?

Activity #2: Get Intentional About Feedback

Identify your preferred method of giving feedback so you can be authentic. Do you prefer handwritten notes, rubrics, one-on-one chats, video feedback, email, or something else? How do you best convey your tone? What interpersonal skills do you have (or lack)?

Acknowledge *their* preferred method of receiving feedback, as well. Know your audience and adapt your delivery to the needs of the person. Different people need, want, and respond better to different types of feedback. Consider when to use:

- The soft touch
- Tactful direct and to-the-point feedback
- Indirect comments
- Blunt, honest (perhaps harsh) critique
- Firm, authoritarian review

I provide the clearest feedback when:

I provide the fastest feedback when:

The best overall method for me:

Recognize and Give Praise to Others in a Way Meaningful to Them

Practice gratitude and constantly remind others of their value to keep them motivated, engaged, and positive. Use these activities to build confidence, reduce stress, and let people know that they're noticed and appreciated, and you'll keep momentum positive during your projects.

> "A person who feels appreciated will always do more than expected."
> —Anonymous

Activity #1: Start a Gratitude Challenge

Day #1	Day #2	Day #3	Day #4	Day #5
Journal about gratitude for five minutes a day for one week. See how it makes you feel.	Deploy your compliment ninjas. Empower students to leave notes for others without being caught.	Make a list of what you are grateful for in your life.	Try a random act of kindness. If needed, look up a kindness bingo board for inspiration.	Get others on board the gratitude train. Have them try out a gratitude activity.
Has your perspective started to shift?	Join in: Compliment and give words of kindness to students and colleagues.	How do you feel as you look at your list?	What did you do? How do you feel? How can you spread more kindness?	What did you try? How did others react? How can you help them *own* gratitude?

Activity #2: Provide the Right Incentives

The first step to motivating people is to *listen*. You need to understand people's why: What makes them want to work on a project or learn something new? Not everyone has had the chance to reflect on what motivates them, so give them the opportunity to tell you what incentives they prefer.

> Research confirms that gratitude improves well-being both mentally and physically. When you practice gratitude, you get healthier *and* contribute to the well-being of those around you.

Present a quick checklist to see what motivates them to complete a task:

- ☐ Makes an impact
- ☐ A challenge
- ☐ Money
- ☐ Good grade/score
- ☐ Instagrammable
- ☐ It's required
- ☐ Sense of completion
- ☐ Award/certificate
- ☐ Chance to connect with people
- ☐ Healthy competition
- ☐ Praise (from a parent, colleague)
- ☐ I care about it
- ☐ I find it interesting
- ☐ Other: _____

Activity #3: Show Gratitude and Praise in Meaningful Ways

We all have different ways of feeling appreciated and valued. Learning new things and taking on projects can be draining. Help others keep their momentum through targeted praise. Ever heard of the five love languages, based on the book by Gary Chapman? These help us tap into the different ways people like to receive praise and gratitude—and some of them may have been completely foreign to us until we learned about them.

Online quizzes abound, but here is a quick overview:

The Five Love Languages
(or The Five Love Languages of School)

1. Words of Affirmation: A special note, kind words, or public acknowledgment
2. Acts of Service: Doing something special just for them
3. Receiving Gifts: Prizes or tokens of appreciation
4. Quality Time: A special event, lunch together, or an outing
5. Physical Touch: A hug, a high-five, or a handshake

Think of individuals you work with (students, colleagues, other adults) and how they might like to receive praise. How will you discover the way each person prefers to receive praise? How will you make that praise authentic?

Authentic Praise Tracker

Name	LL	Ideas for Praise

Manage Expectations and Stress

These activities are all about making and keeping life a little less complicated. Stress tends to flare when expectations aren't met or people don't understand what they're supposed to be doing. Planning and prep can help to avoid those feelings.

Activity #1: Make Expectations Clear

It's easy to feel like you are being clear; after all, you know what you mean. Take time to honestly reflect on how you manage expectations for:

	Notes/Reflection/Ideas
Delivery. When you give directions or explain tasks, ask your listener(s) to regurgitate them back to you. Are they saying what you wanted to hear? If not, it's not them. This might be a sign you need to flesh out what you're asking for or reframe what you expect so others understand.	
Pacing. Are you realistic about what can be accomplished during a given time frame? Try not to overload people. Respect that we all have busy lives and need breaks. People perform their best when they have adequate time to devote to their work.	
Capacity. Emphasize growth over perfection. Realize that people are working within their capacity. Be realistic about what people can achieve, given their abilities. Aim to give them a high yet achievable standard.	
Accessibility. Have you given people opportunities to reach you for input or to express their feelings? Knowing that you're present and are there to support them can go a long way toward relieving tensions.	

Activity #2: Nix the Competitive Atmosphere

We live in a highly competitive world, one in which stress, anxiety, and even busy bragging has become somewhat of a norm. Don't let competitiveness kill your school culture.

Here's a quick checklist to help nix the competitive atmosphere and build community:

☐ Encourage people to *stop* comparing themselves to others. We're all winners when we remember we each bring special and unique qualities to the table. Our only goal should be to be our best selves.

☐ Be an ear. The busy syndrome can be a signal that people are overwhelmed. Maybe they have too much going on, or they're dealing with heavy issues that make them feel like they're in over their head. You don't need to solve it for them, but listening and supporting can go a long way.

☐ Make sure people feel validated. Sometimes people equate being busy with being important.

☐ Validate their real contributions so they don't feel the need to be everything to everyone. Praise is a good way to do this!

☐ Help people get out of the hamster wheel. Before adding more work, make sure people have the capacity to do more. If possible, help others figure out initiatives and tasks they can get rid of so they're not overwhelmed.

☐ Emphasize that failure is okay. If people are afraid to fail or fear they will be judged, they won't accomplish anything. Help others embrace failure as a learning tool, and model how to fail forward.

Inspirational Motivation:
Engage others to be a part of your work

 Checklist: Boosting Inspirational Motivation

Take a moment to reflect on the following leadership strategies and see if any apply to your work.

I want to uncover more ways to:

- Ensure I'm prioritizing impact over ego. Go to page 160.
- Understand my purpose. Go to page 161.
- Establish clear goals that align to my purpose and vision. Go to page 163.
- Engage others in my work. Go to page 164.
- Communicate well. Go to page 169.

 These skills build on each other. While you can jump to whichever section you like, we recommend working through this module in sequential order.

This section is about sharing your vision and goals clearly so others want to engage in your ideas or work. Life is busy, and people are constantly pulled in many directions. Use these strategies to effectively communicate to people why your initiatives add value to *their* lives.

Step 1: Prioritize Impact Over Ego

This section is about staying focused on the real end goal of any problem-solving work. It's natural to want to create, to do your own thing, and to do it for your own reasons. It can be tempting to want credit for your efforts, but it's best if you step back and figure out how to create the biggest impact.

Activity #1: Maximize Your Impact

First things first. Before diving into your own thing, make sure your idea will have the maximum impact by taking time to investigate whether it's even worth pursuing.

> Leading isn't about being the spokesperson; it's about helping to make the end goal possible. Sometimes it means monitoring, sometimes it's providing extra support, and sometimes it's backing away. If you do a great job, the idea spreads—not a person's name.

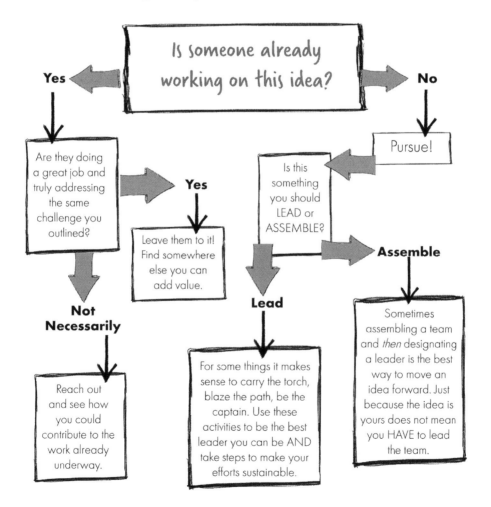

Step 2: Understand Your Purpose and Vision

Use these activities to help you clarify and focus your ideas, your why. Don't make others assemble the vision; give it to them. Everyone is busy with their own goals, dreams, and objectives, so make it clear why they should care about *your* idea/work. Use these activities to help you articulate your why so others understand what you want to do and see the value of taking part in your journey.

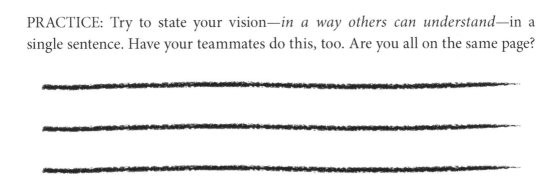

Activity #1: The One-Liner Challenge

If you want others to jump on board with any project, initiative, or lesson, you'll get more buy-in if you can clearly communicate what you want to achieve. While you're brainstorming, it's fine for ideas to be all over the place (it's good, actually), but when you're asking people to invest their time and energy, you need to clearly articulate your what (*project name*) and why (*solution statement*).

PRACTICE: Try to state your vision—*in a way others can understand*—in a single sentence. Have your teammates do this, too. Are you all on the same page?

_____

_____

_____

Saying your idea in one sentence is much more effective than talking it out for five minutes. The more concise you are with your goal, the more likely you are to achieve it.

Activity #2: What's Your Story?

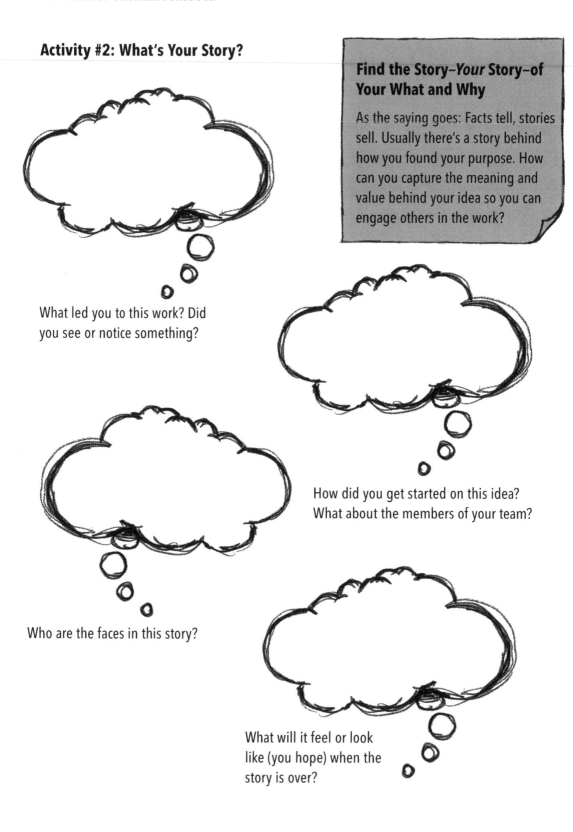

Find the Story–*Your* Story–of Your What and Why

As the saying goes: Facts tell, stories sell. Usually there's a story behind how you found your purpose. How can you capture the meaning and value behind your idea so you can engage others in the work?

What led you to this work? Did you see or notice something?

How did you get started on this idea? What about the members of your team?

Who are the faces in this story?

What will it feel or look like (you hope) when the story is over?

Step 3: Establish Clear Goals That Align to Your Purpose and Vision

Get Creative

Sketch

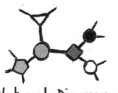

Network Diagram

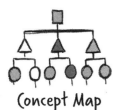

Concept Map

Decision Tree

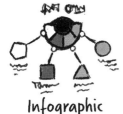

Infographic

This activity will help you visualize your plan and see how it connects to your greater educational vision. Good leaders think about the big picture and inspire teammates with their vision and ability to put the pieces together. The more structure and clarity you can provide, the better, as aimlessness can lead to frustration, stagnation, and the possible demise of your work. Break your vision into individual pieces. Lay them out. Are you prioritizing the actions and goals that will help you achieve your vision?

Activity #1: Visualize Your Goals

We love visualizing. Why? It helps us think through the nitty-gritty of what we want to do *and* gives us a vision to present to others. Whether it's a drawing, a chart, a roadmap, a storyboard, or whatever else you choose, make sure you lay out the pieces and show how they connect.

Step 4: Engage Others in Your Work

This section is all about packaging your idea to show its value. Do this to:

1. Get the green light you need to get started.

2. Engage others to jump on board or support your work.

Pitching has a variety of formats. It may be an informal chat with your peers, a quick elevator pitch at the staff meeting, or a pitch deck (slide presentation) you share with administration or other potential allies. Whatever it is, it must evolve as your project evolves. Unlike a normal presentation, your message should shift depending on who you are trying to engage. What you focus on for administration may be slightly different than gathering your colleagues' support (same goes for parents and your students). Shifting your pitch accordingly helps ensure you get the engagement and support you seek.

> Everyone is busy and has their own goals and dreams, so why should they work with you or even care about *yours*?

> What is a pitch? It's an overview of your idea to get others to invest resources (e.g., time, money, support, supplies) in your project.

Activity #1: Pitch Perfect

You're ready to get support for your work, share it with your peers, set up a meeting with your principal, or present it for a minute in an upcoming staff meeting. Now it's all about sharing the right angle for the audience. Follow this simple pitch deck to craft your main points or perfect that elevator pitch to get the green light for your project and support for your idea.

Dealing with rejection:

Don't take it personally if people aren't interested in your work. It may be a sign that you need to improve upon the idea. Educators are often encouraged to give up on their ideas if they don't work out the first time. That's not how innovation works. Learn from every rejection and figure out how to regroup and move forward. We want our students to learn from failure, so we must practice it for ourselves.

The Pitch Deck: Our universal how-to guide for your pitching needs.

Overall rule: Less is more! Be clear and concise because you only have a few minutes to truly capture someone's interest.

You Say hello and introduce yourself:	**The Problem/Opportunity** What are you working to address? Tell a story, if you can (and we mean tell, don't type any of it into your slide). 30 Seconds!	**The Solution** How do you plan to address the problem? (Think solution statement.)
ADAPT TO YOUR AUDIENCE: If people don't know you, add your title and contact information.	ADAPT TO YOUR AUDIENCE: Use your story work! Paint a picture to pull at those heart strings.	ADAPT TO YOUR AUDIENCE: Replace any jargon or 'teacher speak' as needed.
The Value What will this project achieve? For whom?	**The Plan** Share need-to-know logistics. What are the big steps and timelines? What resources are needed?	**The Ask** How can your audience support you and your work?
ADAPT FOR YOUR AUDIENCE: Which impact(s) most align with their motives and goals? Share the benefits that would most appeal to your audience.	ADAPT FOR YOUR AUDIENCE: Be strategic here. Don't waste time. If you need something specific that your audience might have, highlight that.	ADAPT FOR YOUR AUDIENCE: Provide a clear ask of what you want them to DO. And of course: Say thank you.

Activity #2: Go TED Talk Style

What we've learned from TED Talks is that there is no message so important that it can't be communicated in fifteen minutes or less. That's the beauty of the TED Talk: The speaker has carefully crafted what they want to say in an enticing and concise manner. Isn't that what we should try to do with our own messages?

How can you use this same structure to communicate key ideas with and for students?

Decide on your message.

After people hear your talk, how would they describe it to others? Keep in mind they'll probably do this in only one sentence. What do you want that sentence to be? (E.g., "They gave strategies on how we could use technology in a meaningful way.")

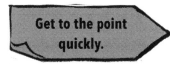
Hook them.

Tell a story, do an interactive activity, give a message that creates an aha moment. Whatever you think will draw them in and help you connect.

Get to the point quickly.

Giving a talk is not about going through mundane details. In fact, people are usually better off reading the details for themselves. Make your message clear, connect with the audience, and focus on giving them something to think about–and do it quickly.

Make your idea sticky.

As educators, we spend every day trying to make students care about the ideas we're sharing. How can you ensure your idea makes a lasting impression?

Be authentic.

When you're speaking about a topic you're passionate about, it's obvious. Use that natural energy to ignite the room.

Activity #3: Be Realistic: Tip Sheet

We're all bombarded with new ideas and information. Make it easier for people to understand why they should pay attention to what *you're* offering by being strategic about how you share information.

Keep It Relevant

Remember that everyone's busy, and you need to be explicit when you explain why this idea is more important or relevant than other ideas. Only then will they be more likely to prioritize it.

1. Be clear with how your idea is relevant *to them.*

2. Be clear with your ask. What exactly do you want them to do or contribute?

3. Be explicit about the benefits of your idea. How will this idea connect to their work and help them achieve their goals?

KISS
(Keep It Simple, Stupid)

Ever heard of the curse of knowledge? It's when you know so much about a topic that it becomes hard for you to decipher between what tidbits people need to know and what's extraneous fluff. Keep people engaged and avoid a volcanic eruption of information overload. Get to the core idea people need to know or understand to engage in your work.

Activity #4: Shifting from My Vision to Our Vision

Quick checks:

- Are you telling people what to do or are you including them in the dialogue?
- When people take on tasks, are you providing space for them to take charge (e.g., letting them run, innovate, or design a portion of the project)?
- Has your vision evolved as you've gathered more team members? How have you been able to integrate the ideas of others into the vision?

When people feel like they have part ownership of an idea or project, and they choose to invest time in it, they're more likely to embrace it and take it further than you could have taken it alone.

Step Four Reflection

List at least three actionable to-dos to engage others in your work.

Step 5: Practice Your Communication

As educators, we practice public speaking every day, but that doesn't mean we stop learning. Take time to make sure you're effectively communicating what you want. Use these activities to reflect on your delivery and make sure you're achieving the desired effect with your words. Whether it's to get buy-in for an idea or to manage conflicts between team members, *how* you say things can be more important than *what* you say.

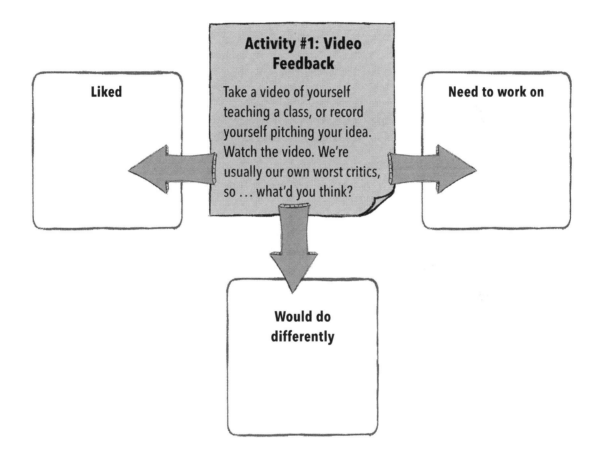

Activity #2: Practice the Art of Negotiation

You're probably negotiating daily: What to eat for dinner, why your child should put their toys away, why students should take that next assessment seriously. Maybe you haggled for a great deal for your new car or solved a family crisis. Think of your most recent negotiation:

What strategies did you use?

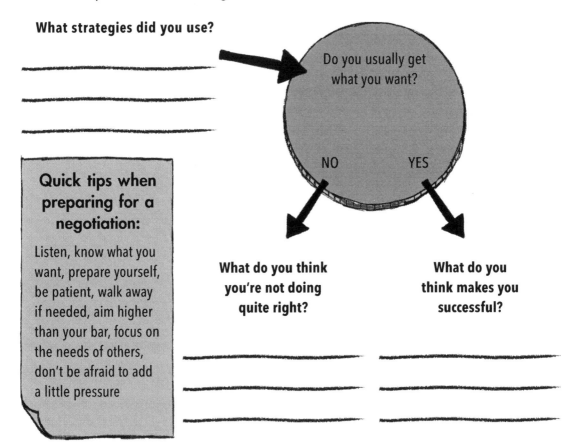

Quick tips when preparing for a negotiation:

Listen, know what you want, prepare yourself, be patient, walk away if needed, aim higher than your bar, focus on the needs of others, don't be afraid to add a little pressure

Do you usually get what you want?

NO   YES

What do you think you're not doing quite right?

What do you think makes you successful?

Activity #3: Practice Your Perfect Email

Let's face it: Email is an essential means of communication. It has also become a daily time-suck that forces us to sift through dozens of messages each day. Knowing all that, how do you motivate others to read your email, let alone respond to it? How can you rise above the noise and increase your chances of a positive response?

> We've all seen what happens when our students can't effectively communicate. Strive to set the bar high. You're more likely to meet your objectives, and you'll model a crucial skill to students.

PRACTICE YOUR PERFECT EMAIL

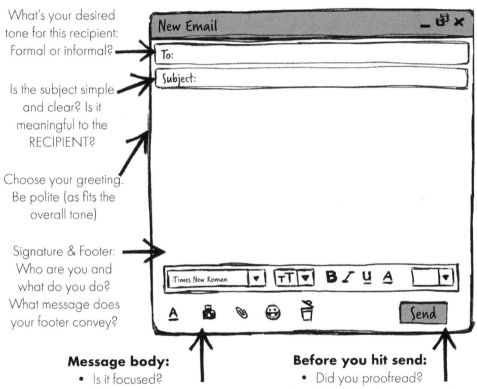

What's your desired tone for this recipient: Formal or informal?

Is the subject simple and clear? Is it meaningful to the RECIPIENT?

Choose your greeting. Be polite (as fits the overall tone)

Signature & Footer: Who are you and what do you do? What message does your footer convey?

Message body:
- Is it focused?
- Have you used the fewest words possible to say what is needed to say RIGHT NOW?
- Is your purpose clear?
- Is your request clear?
- Have you made it as easy as possible for them to say yes?

Before you hit send:
- Did you proofread?
- Is there someone else you trust who can read to check your tone and content?
- Is it sharable? (*Don't write anything you wouldn't want others to see.*)

Intellectual Stimulation:
Tap into the talent that surrounds you

Checklist: Boosting Intellectual Stimulation
Take a moment to reflect on the following leadership strategies and see if any apply to your work.

I want to uncover more ways to:

- Create a safe space where we can explore new ideas and different perspectives without judgment or humiliation. Go to page 173.

- Offer opportunities for others to explore and play with new ideas, subjects, and connections. Go to page 177.

- Facilitate activities or exercises that allow people to expand their thinking. Go to page 178.

- Encourage everyone to push each other to reach their potential. Go to page 179.

- Help everyone see the big picture. Go to page 180.

Use this section to spark curiosity in others. Good leaders assume the best in people and trust them to find solutions to challenges. Use these strategies to help others realize their full potential by uncovering ways to work *with* others so they are inspired to engage in your work and push ideas forward.

Create a Safe Space

Create a safe space where exploration can happen without judgment or humiliation. Part of leading a great team and motivating others (in the classroom or on a project) is making sure people feel comfortable where they are, with each other, with themselves, and with you. Create a space where they want to be, and where they trust that their diverse perspectives will be heard and valued. The more people are willing to share without fear, the further you will take ideas and projects.

Activity #1: Set the Scene

We talk a lot about redesigning learning spaces, but focus now on the way the classroom or meeting space *feels* instead of just how it looks. Yes, there is overlap.

- Does your space feel warm and inviting? Does it feel homey to you? To students? To colleagues?

- Can you play with the design of your space?

- Can you bring in more color and natural light?

- Can you use music or sound to make it more inviting?

- Can you use movement to make people comfortable?

- Can you, where appropriate, take it outside?

- Can there be food and beverages?

- Can you change the locale every once in a while (use the theater or media center, that nice coffee shop, or the new makerspace)?

The highest need is for the space to be safe—for ideas, for sharing, for failing. And that takes time, repetition, and you. You set the tone for your space.

Sketch

Activity #2: Draw Your Ideal Space

Use images, adjectives, and ideas to brainstorm the space you would most enjoy, for you and for others.

Activity #3: Self-Reflections to Foster a Safe Space

		Write it in your own words:
Don't make assumptions about actions.	Ask. Listen. Ask. Listen. Don't guess people's motives. If you're unsure about why something happened or why someone said a certain thing or acted a certain way, ask. Reach out. Always assume the best first.	I need to / I will …
Don't make assumptions about ideas.	You can't know what you don't know. We frequently talk about common sense, but just because something seems like common knowledge or practical know-how doesn't mean that's the case for others. Everyone comes from different starting points and sets of experiences. Never assume knowledge.	I need to / I will …
Understand different points of view.	When a person shares something outside of your experience, how do you react? Do you dismiss their experience or ask for more details? How well can you step into someone else's shoes and see or feel their perspective?	I need to / I will …
Monitor reactions.	Can you keep a calm face? Can you disagree without raising your voice? Without insulting? Interrupting? Can you walk away from a debate and not hold a grudge or take it personally?	I need to / I will …
Build connections and interactions.	Do you encourage deep dialogues that allow people to express their point of view and get to know one another? Do you take an active role in facilitating those connections?	I need to / I will …
Keep communication open.	This is about others knowing when and how to reach you. Are you able to take time for issues that people clearly want to discuss? Even if it feels off-task?	I need to / I will …
Clear the air.	If you want to keep things going, you may have to address the elephant in the room before you can move forward. Are you aware when there's an uncomfortable weight? How do you clear that tension away?	I need to / I will …

Activity #4: Allow People to Express Themselves

You must increase opportunities to hear all voices and provide a variety of outlets that encourage engagement and capture insights from your whole team. People communicate in different ways and with different conditions. Find ways to hear everyone's two cents and you will benefit your team and your project.

Day to Day

Easier said than done, but try not to let the people who speak the loudest dominate the conversation. Find ways to capture and elevate every voice (introverts, we've got your back!). We all know raising hands doesn't spread the love. Here are a few of our favorite ways to provide opportunities for individual reflection and input.

↓

Write it. Get creative with notecards, Post-its, and entry/exit tickets. Give people time to jot down their reflections before or after a group activity.

↓

Use structured conversation. Fishbowls, conversation menus, small groups, debates, and assigned role play (see Module Five) help more individuals join in the discussion.

↓

Tech it up. Help people engage with virtual posting boards, video responses (Flipgrid), real-time polls, interactive presentations (Nearpod, PearDeck), and backchannels.

↓

Provide feedback opportunities.
Sometimes people have a lot they want to say, but don't want to share in front of everyone. Emails, surveys, office hours, and response cards provide a great outlet for people to put in their two cents without the pressure of a group.

Assessments and Final Deliverables

Get creative with how you assess. You don't always have to pick the type of deliverable (e.g., a research paper or poster) that students need to create to demonstrate their mastery. Same goes for any problem-solving initiative. Provide as much choice as possible for people to package their work.

↓

Written. Think journals, reports, essays, blogs, and poems.

↓

Oral. Think speeches, presentations, vlogs, and debates.

↓

Visual: Think poster, collage, video, or drawing.

Artistic: Think performance, song, or artwork.

↓

Technology. Create a mock website, allow people to use an app or software you've never heard of (Comic Strip Maker, Storyboard, Puppet Show, etc.), or use Google Suite. Use tech to enhance any of these options! Let others show you which tools they love.

Offer Opportunities for Others to Explore and Play with New Ideas, Subjects, and Connections

This is all about figuring out how others can tap into their own creativity. While you can't force creativity, you can encourage people to rest their minds and provide time to let their thoughts wander.

Activity #1: Making Time for Creativity (in the Classroom and Conference Room)

Down Time/Free Time. Give people the opportunity to do nothing. Encourage them to soak up the world and think freely. Staying busy all the time prevents us from exploring random thoughts, ideas, and tangents. When we have nothing to do, that's when our mind is most free to explore ideas.	**Outside Time.** Use any chance to go outside. Nature increases happiness and keeps your brain fresh. It inspires and enhances your creativity. Don't get stuck, get out. Even a simple walk can do a world of good.	**Move It Minutes.** Take a few minutes to get oxygen flowing to the brain and wake up. Stretch, stand, or shift your seated discussion to a cocktail hour mixer. Moving is a great way to get the creative juices flowing.
Reflection Minutes. Take a moment to pause and let people digest information and make connections. If you ask them what they think, be patient. Wait. Give them time to gather their thoughts and formulate them.	**Play Time.** Why does play time stop after kindergarten? Everyone needs time to play with new ideas, new tools, new resources, and new people. Help stimulate ideas by giving people the chance to tinker and get their hands dirty.	**Excursion Time.** Get out. Explore. Take mini field trips. Use a different space. Changing up the location and seeing what's out there can generate new ideas and different perspectives.
Genius Hour. Devote a set time for people to work on activities of personal interest. Building in time for people to invest energy in their interests and passions can take their thinking to the next level.	**Rest Time.** Give people time to relax and take a break. They'll come back refreshed. It could be a few minutes to put their heads down or time to drink their coffee in peace. People need that chance to unplug and recharge.	**Mindfulness Minutes.** Take a few moments for well-being. Use meditation to relieve stress. Take deep breaths to relieve tension. Make sure those you're working with are in a good place mentally and, if not, give them the opportunity to find their equilibrium.

Facilitate Activities and Exercises that Encourage People to Expand Their Thinking

This section is all about setting a high yet achievable bar to help people reach their creative potential. Use these activities to help others expand their thinking and develop ideas to solve challenges that arise.

Activity #1: The Creativity Sampler

Create challenging experiences so others can achieve higher levels of performance.

Brainstorming Activities. Spark curiosity through collaboration. See Module Five for a variety of ideas.

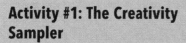

Deep Dialogues. Uncover new perspectives that expand your mind and creative potential. Use activities from Module Five to set the stage for individuals to share, converse with, and learn from one another.

PBL It. PBL isn't only for students. Enable your team to explore challenges and develop solutions as you would for a classroom PBL.

Simulations. Create a real-world experience. Set the scene and let people role play. This is a great way to gain empathy about a situation and insights into a problem.

Make It. Tinker, build, and explore. Provide any available resources and see what happens when teams take on the makerspace mentality.

Consulting Projects. Give individuals or teams the problem and the resources needed to solve the problem. Then give them freedom to find their own process, create a plan, and package their end product as they see fit.

Activity #2: Tips to Encourage Autonomy

- **Assume the Best.** If you trust your team, show it. Give them responsibility and set accountability checks. Help them to own their success (and failure).

- **Set a High Bar and Achievable Target with Clear Expectations.** Make the end product clear, as well as any goals you'd like to accomplish. This allows others to own the process while striving for high quality.

- **Involve Others in Decision-Making.** Ownership over ideas makes people feel valued. Look for opportunities to include others in big and little decisions so they have a stake in what's happening.

- **Let Them Set the Pace.** It's okay to create a deadline, but allow people to set their own schedule for when and how they'll get their work done.

- **Provide Support for Working Through Trouble Spots.** Support does not mean giving someone the solution. Take time to show, model, and guide people through tough spots so they learn how to find the answer for themselves.

Encourage Collaboration

These activities focus on ways to encourage your team members to push each other to reach their highest, fullest potential. Any group or project work will falter in a spirit of competition or jealousy. Everyone wins when one person hits on a great idea, so nurture a supportive collaborative environment and avoid potential pettiness and cliques.

Define. Work together to define what you expect from one another. Example: Be supportive, reliable, respectful, committed, honest, _____...

**Activity #1:
Be a Team Player**

Part of stimulating people to find solutions or push their thinking is to encourage them to work together effectively.

Encourage. Show gratitude, give credit where credit is due, and empower people to activate great ideas.

Listen and Question. Actively listen to others, promote dialogue, welcome questions, and question what isn't clear. Your goal as a team is to support each another and take your ideas further. You cannot do that on assumptions.

Create Accountability. Make collaboration a part of an assessment or evaluation. Make sure people know that how you treat others is just as important as the end product.

Activity #2: Feedback That Pushes Thinking

Steps to provide others with constructive feedback:

- [ ] **Highlight Assumptions:** Ask people to validate why they think an idea would or wouldn't work.
- [ ] **"What If" Input:** Use your expertise to offer new ideas, but frame them in a way that allows others to own the ideas themselves.
- [ ] **Turn Problems Into Opportunities:** Help others find the positive or opportunity in a situation.
- [ ] **Positive Expectations:** Show others that they're capable of achieving whatever goal you've set forth.
- [ ] **Be Concrete:** Provide clear action items or thoughts to consider.

Help people see the big picture!

Education can be a siloed field. Even the way we're told to teach subjects is a bit misleading, as most issues are interdisciplinary, not stand-alone topics. Being effective with our ideas and pushing our thinking requires us to think more holistically about situations and problems so we have a thorough understanding of how to achieve goals and materialize solutions. When you help everyone see the big picture and understand the moving parts at play, you will spark new ideas and better solutions.

Activity #1: Practice Systems Thinking

Think of your school as an ecosystem or machine. Draw a diagram labeling the interconnected pieces or moving parts.

Systems thinking means understanding how things are interrelated and how they influence one another. It's a way to see the big picture.

Activity #2: Encourage Systems Thinking

Review your ecosystem (above). What systems are at play that allow (or prevent) your school to run (or not) efficiently? Label your drawing (above). Then answer the questions on the left.

Help Others Identify Systems. Define the system you're working within.

Visualize the System. Make it feel tangible by drawing it out.

Change the System. Explore cause and effect. If you change one part of the system, what's the ripple effect?

Explore the System. Understand the moving parts at play and how they're interconnected.

181

Idealized Influence
Be the change you want to see

Checklist: Boosting Idealized Influence

Take a moment to reflect on the following leadership strategies and see if any apply to your work.

I want to uncover more ways to:

- Manage emotions. Go to page 183.

- Ditch drama. Go to page 187.

- Strive to be a good role model in all aspects. Go to page 192.

- Be authentic; ensure people are comfortable with me. Go to page 193.

- Live my ethics and values. Go to page 194.

- Gain trust and respect because people know they can rely on me. Go to page 197.

> This section is all about walking the talk and leading by example. It's about modeling your ethics and values and contributing toward a positive school culture. Use these strategies to make sure you're exemplifying the type of leader you want to be.

Manage Emotions

This section is about taking charge of your thoughts and feelings. Innovating and problem-solving aren't easy, but it is easy to get upset when people question our ideas or don't understand what we're talking about. This is why we must learn to temper our reactions. Remember: you're learning. It's no one's fault (not yours or theirs) if someone doesn't like or "get" what you're trying to do. It's a chance for you to truly listen to what people are telling you and learn from their insights.

We often call this "learning from failure," but it's not failure. It's a journey. Try out an idea, learn from your experience and what others tell you, and repeat until you get there. The biggest obstacle is usually your own mindset.

Activity #1: Rationalize It!

The best leaders focus on the goal, the solution, and the end target. This is valuable on many fronts, but mostly because it helps us stay rational and invest our time and energy in how we can accomplish the task to the best of our abilities. Remember, when you get feedback, it's not a personal attack. You don't need to put up your guard! It's natural to get defensive when we feel rejected, but if you rationalize what's happening and understand how to use these invaluable insights, you can make your ideas even better.

Here are the most common ways of improving upon your idea using feedback. Notice the difference is in your reaction.

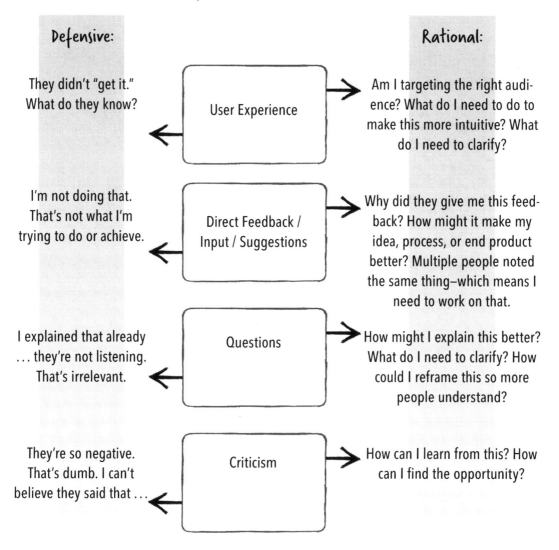

Defensive:

They didn't "get it." What do they know?

I'm not doing that. That's not what I'm trying to do or achieve.

I explained that already … they're not listening. That's irrelevant.

They're so negative. That's dumb. I can't believe they said that …

Rational:

Am I targeting the right audience? What do I need to do to make this more intuitive? What do I need to clarify?

Why did they give me this feedback? How might it make my idea, process, or end product better? Multiple people noted the same thing–which means I need to work on that.

How might I explain this better? What do I need to clarify? How could I reframe this so more people understand?

How can I learn from this? How can I find the opportunity?

User Experience

Direct Feedback / Input / Suggestions

Questions

Criticism

Activity #2: Tips for Dealing with Toxic People

Sure, good leaders rationalize criticism (see Activity #1), but let's face it, people can be unpleasant. Don't let them get the better of you. Here are our favorite suggestions for dealing with toxic people.

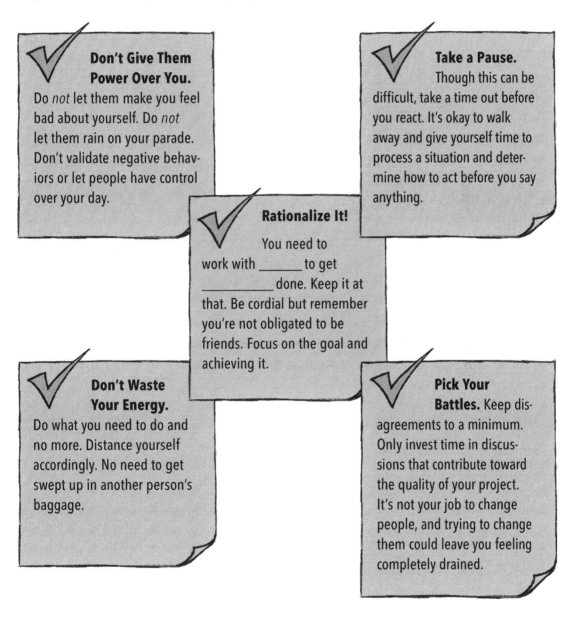

Don't Give Them Power Over You.
Do *not* let them make you feel bad about yourself. Do *not* let them rain on your parade. Don't validate negative behaviors or let people have control over your day.

Take a Pause.
Though this can be difficult, take a time out before you react. It's okay to walk away and give yourself time to process a situation and determine how to act before you say anything.

Rationalize It!
You need to work with _____ to get _____ done. Keep it at that. Be cordial but remember you're not obligated to be friends. Focus on the goal and achieving it.

Don't Waste Your Energy.
Do what you need to do and no more. Distance yourself accordingly. No need to get swept up in another person's baggage.

Pick Your Battles. Keep disagreements to a minimum. Only invest time in discussions that contribute toward the quality of your project. It's not your job to change people, and trying to change them could leave you feeling completely drained.

Activity #3: Leave Personal Baggage at the Door

We all need a shoulder to lean on sometimes, but it's also important not to overshare. Life can become so draining that it prevents us from getting things done. Try these strategies to manage tough emotions:

Reframe your mood

Try to replace bad or sad thoughts with positive ones. Before you get too deep into a mood, see if you can hold onto a moment, a video, or anything to lighten your mind.

Learn what makes you tick. You'll be better prepared to deal with and navigate away from instances that might get you upset.

Know your emotional triggers

Find a healthy outlet

Do you like to run? Read poetry? Whatever your outlet is to help you deal with negative emotions and stress, make time to employ it as often as possible.

Go to Module Four for ideas about how to take care of yourself.

Take time for self-care

Ditch Drama

This section is all about creating a positive atmosphere so people can focus on solutions rather than problems.

We've been inspired by Cy Wakeman and her reality-based research with The Futures Company, which found that the average employee wastes over two hours each day on drama. We don't know what that number is for the average teacher, but it sounds about right to us. Use these activities to help alleviate drama from your work so you can get stuff done with less stress.

Activity #1: Ditch Drama Bingo Board

Make a conscious choice to *not* engage in the drama, and take steps to avoid it.

Activity #2: Help People Manage Change

Change can be scary. People try to resist it and get angry about it, but ultimately change happens. Help them through the process.

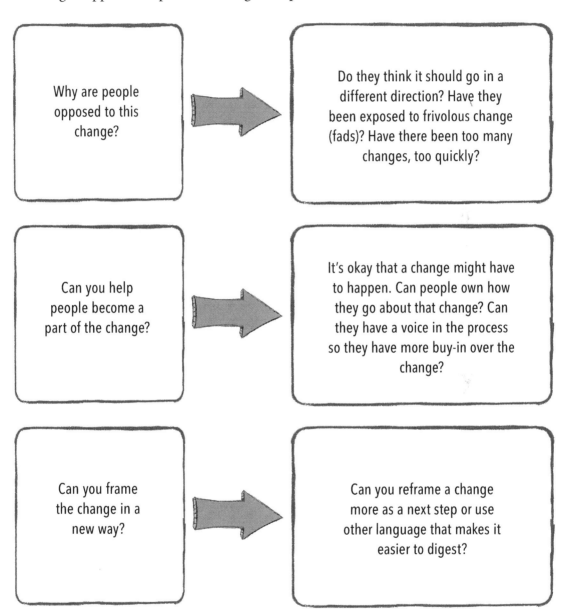

Why are people opposed to this change?

Do they think it should go in a different direction? Have they been exposed to frivolous change (fads)? Have there been too many changes, too quickly?

Can you help people become a part of the change?

It's okay that a change might have to happen. Can people own how they go about that change? Can they have a voice in the process so they have more buy-in over the change?

Can you frame the change in a new way?

Can you reframe a change more as a next step or use other language that makes it easier to digest?

Activity #3: Don't Waste People's Time

Seems like this should go without saying, but we all know people who need to hear this. Model how you would like to be treated.

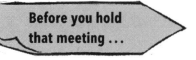

Know what you want to achieve. Nothing frustrates people more than a pointless meeting. If you don't have clear goals or a clear agenda, it's probably not a necessary meeting. If it's only to share information, perhaps there's another outlet that can better serve your purpose and save others' time.

- Can you share in an email?
- Can you pass along your PowerPoint?
- Can you use a virtual platform to stay in touch (Drive, Slack, Voxer)?

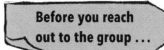

One person "acts up"—and we all know who—and the leader sends a group email. It's not discreet. It starts a chain of time-wasting drama. Know when to reach out individually and when to be inclusive. For critiques or praise, it's not always necessary to get everyone involved. Sometimes it's best to try a one-on-one meeting, a phone call, an email, a note, a Voxer message, or something else discreet and personal. This lets the person you're reaching out to know you respect their privacy without wasting other people's time or causing drama.

Know when to lead and when to collaborate. Collaborating is great, but be real about your intentions. There's no sense collaborating for the sake of collaborating when you already know what you want people to do or work on. People get frustrated when they're pulled into meetings to discuss ideas, only to find out that their efforts will go nowhere, so be honest with yourself before running a planning session and clarify why you are calling people together.

- Are you trying to identify a problem to address together? If you already have an idea of what the problem is, don't waste people's time brainstorming problems, hoping they come up with the same problem as you. Just tell them, "_____ is a problem" and work together to find a solution. Which brings us to …

- Do you want people to develop their own solutions or do you want their help implementing your idea? Again, do not waste time workshopping solutions if you already have a solution in mind. Just tell them, "_____ is a problem and I think we should _____." Then you can get their feedback on how best to implement your idea.

This will save a lot of time and frustration.

Strive to Be a Good Role Model in All Aspects

This section is all about walking the talk and practicing what you preach.

Activity #1: Are You Walking the Talk?

Cognitive dissonance means holding contra-dicting views, such as when behavior contra-dicts what you state as your views.

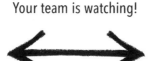

Your team is watching!

Hypocrisy means claiming you believe one thing while saying or doing something to contradict that.

You know those people; they complain about so-and-so gossiping all the time as they gossip. They tell you to take risks, even though they don't take any. Be honest with yourself, and ask folks who know you. Where might you need to be a little more self-aware and up your game?

Activity #2: Be Positive About Yourself

You want every person on your team to have a positive view of themselves, to believe in their potential. Model what this looks like. **More self-care strategies coming up in Module Four!**

- Praise and appreciate yourself.
- Stay humble.
- Don't compare yourself.
- Practice mindfulness.
- Stay kind.
- Love your uniqueness.
- Appreciate your life.
- Own your strengths (and weaknesses).
- Choose happiness.

Be Authentic

This section is about being the true version of you, rather than the version you think others want you to be (and yes, folks can smell the difference).

> Being authentic is not to be confused with over-sharing and unleashing all your personal baggage. It's having the courage to be true to *you*.

Activity #1: Show Your Human Side

Don't be afraid to own your weaknesses. They make you even more likable and relatable. Plus, self-awareness goes a long way toward our own empowerment.

- **Mistakes.** You're going to make them. Own them, learn from them, and move forward.
- **Flaws.** You still can't spell? You trip over your own feet? It's okay. No need to hide, because those are the features that make you more lovable.
- **Weaknesses.** Can't say no when someone asks you to do something? Still have a hard time speaking in front of a room full of adults? No worries; once you recognize those problems, you can develop your capabilities.

Activity #2: Recognize When You're Faking It

You can't lead with conviction if you don't believe in the project. If you want to be authentic, you must be fully invested in the cause. Look for the signs. These are your body's way of telling you something's not quite right:

- Bad feeling in your gut?
- Smile feel plastered?
- Having to convince yourself?
- Feel heavy?
- Trouble sleeping?

If you've got any of these symptoms, reflect on why you're doing what you're doing. If you're working on a project out of obligation or pressure rather than a true desire (and we get it, sometimes that's just life), can you make what you *have* to do align with what you *want* to do? The more you can be true to yourself, the better you will feel and the more productive you will be.

Live Your Ethics and Values

This section is about recognizing and embodying what you believe in. This is one of the best ways to connect your work to your core and make sure the ideas and projects you invest in speak to your belief system.

Activity #1: Define Your Values

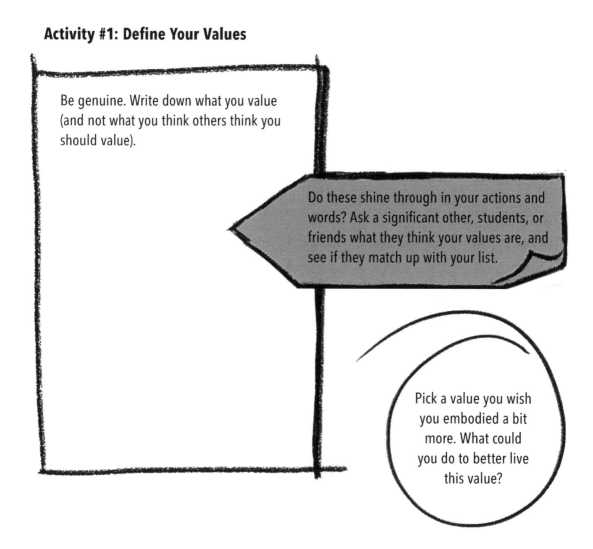

Be genuine. Write down what you value (and not what you think others think you should value).

Do these shine through in your actions and words? Ask a significant other, students, or friends what they think your values are, and see if they match up with your list.

Pick a value you wish you embodied a bit more. What could you do to better live this value?

Activity #2: Effectively Model Your Ethics and Values Through Your Interactions with Others

What code of ethics do you attempt to follow?

Now think through your daily interactions with others. How well do you live out your code? What are you doing well? Where could you improve?

Examples of ethics: respect for others, kindness, dependability, honesty, integrity.

Activity #3: Handling Moral Dilemmas

As teachers, we deal with many issues that wake us up in the night. We're almost always wondering if we did the right thing. If you feel like something is a true disservice to your students or to your peers, don't be afraid to speak up.

Step 1: Stop and assess: You're feeling the warning signs that something is up. Is this a problem? Sometimes situations may flash and in the heat of the moment, feel like a moral issue. But when you give it a day, you realize it's not. So step one, assess: Is this actually a dilemma?

Step 2: Understand your dilemma: What's bothering you about the issue? Clearly identify what's putting you on edge. Then break it down.

- What's the rationale behind what's happening?
- Why did this situation or issue come up in the first place? It might go down differently on paper than in real life. It's important to get to the motivation behind the action or situation that is bothering you. What can you find evidence of, or prove?

- What are the pros and cons of each side?
- Keep this as rational and factual as possible. Don't make assumptions; ask clear questions.

Step 3: Decide whether it's worth taking action

In a case of right versus wrong, it's easy to take action. In education, though, we're often stuck in right versus right dilemmas, where multiple parties think they have students' best interests at heart. So pause and consider:

- Is this something that *needs* to change?
- Is this something *you* can change or influence?
- What is the cost or benefit of action? Of inaction?

For bigger issues–the ones that feel hopeless *(cough cough, policy changes)*–find a way to contribute. Speak up. Write and email, join the protest, vote, go to the board meeting, write a blog, host a meeting, make a call, join an organization, or sign that petition.

For smaller issues, devise a thoughtful strategy. Who do you need to speak with? What's the most tactful way to approach the subject? Provide a path forward.

Step 4: Understand the value of your voice

Big changes–often the most important ones–don't happen overnight. They can take years or decades. The more we understand the dilemma (see also Root Cause, page 84-85), the greater the likelihood we can change the large systems or beliefs. This can feel so big and overwhelming that we give up or become jaded. Please know that even if you can't *be* the solution, you can be a part of it. Let your voice be heard, even if you don't see an immediate impact.

Gain Trust and Respect Because People Know They Can Rely on You

This section is about being the rock and providing the stability that every good initiative needs.

Activity #1: Be Present

Reflect on your actions and resolve to:
- Show up. Are you present when people expect you to be?
- Be on time. Are you ready and prepared for meetings and events?
- Be transparent. Are you keeping everyone in the know? Is your agenda clear?
- Be committed. Are you fully invested in the work?

Half of being a good leader is just showing up. Think about it: How much does it mean to you when people are present—truly present—in your life? When people follow through on obligations, however small? People need to know they can trust you. No one follows a flake. (Might be harsh, but it's true.)

Activity #2: Respect Confidentiality

As with any team, issues will arise, including differences over how much information your team wants to share. We say exercise caution and let your team decide when to offer up information.
- Personal Matters. When people confide in you, assume it is for your ears only.
- Conflict Management. X and Y are in a dispute over how to tackle an issue. Be a neutral mediator and set up a safe space for X and Y to talk it out. Don't turn conflict into a he-said, she-said situation. Instead of getting in the middle, help facilitate a dialogue between the two parties. Don't let the conflict spread.
- Mindful Communication. You know how you don't share information in an email unless it's something you're okay with everyone seeing? Not everyone knows this rule. Don't forward or share information without asking permission.

Activity #3: Be Accountable for Yourself

Accountability is a decision. It's accepting that your actions and decisions have consequences, even if they're not the outcomes you were hoping for. It's easy to blame others when the situation feels out of our control, but this never gets us anywhere. Even if you can't directly change an issue, focus on what you *can* change and control, and put yourself back in the driver's seat. You have more power over your life than you think.

How accountable do you hold yourself?

- How often do you play victim?
- How often do you own negative results?
- How often do you come up with excuses for your shortcomings?
- How often do you say "What can I do differently"?

"Life is 10 percent what happens to you and 90 percent how you react to it." – Charles R. Swindoll

I was once at a conference where a speaker was going over the mentality behind bad test scores. In some countries, individuals were more likely to blame external factors for a bad test score (e.g., bad teachers, too few resources). In other countries, individuals were more likely to blame themselves (e.g., they hadn't studied enough or put in enough effort). What was fascinating was that the cultures where people took ownership of their shortcomings were more likely to improve than the cultures were students were more likely to blame external factors. Which category do you fall in?

Activity #4: The Platinum Rule

The Golden Rule is a classic, and a great general rule of thumb, but the Platinum Rule will help you gain insights on how others want to be treated.

We all want ideals like fairness, consistency, and recognition, but what those look like in action may vary greatly from person to person.

Consider how we show appreciation for others:
- *Golden Rule:* You love big celebrations so you host elaborate festivities to show your appreciation.
- *Platinum Rule:* Others do not enjoy big celebrations or being the center of attention. Teacher X would simply prefer a thank you and a gift card, while Teacher Y would feel most loved with a handwritten note.

The Platinum Rule: Do unto others what they want us to do unto them.

The Platinum Rule can help you be a better leader on many levels.

Where, when, and with whom will you apply the Platinum Rule?

Final Thoughts: Reflections on Your Leadership

You are a leader. Full stop. If you don't yet see yourself as such, keep coming back to this section to practice and hone your leadership skills. While you can certainly execute the Educator Canvas solo and make an impact, when you cultivate yourself as a leader, you will be able to achieve so much more. As you wrap up Module Three, reflect on your work.

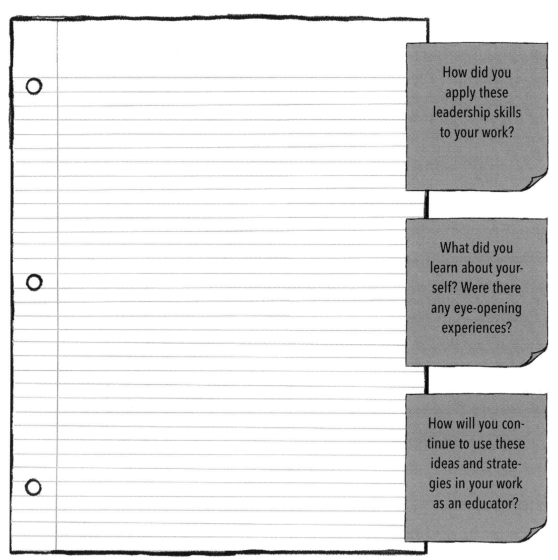

How did you apply these leadership skills to your work?

What did you learn about yourself? Were there any eye-opening experiences?

How will you continue to use these ideas and strategies in your work as an educator?

practice
and **hone** your
leadership
skills

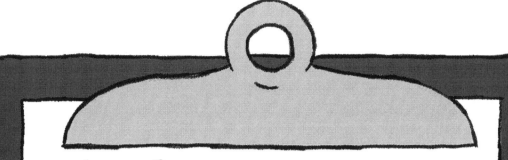

Module Four:

Startup Your Mental Stamina:

Self-Care Strategies to Prevent Burnout

In this module:

- The mental game behind teaching
- Our story behind self-care: The importance of preventing burnout
- Tap into your strengths: Recharge, refresh, repeat
- Activities to focus on self-care:
  - ▸ Heart: What do I care about? Why am I doing this?
  - ▸ Optimism: Yes! Change is possible
  - ▸ Curiosity: You're a lifelong learner
  - ▸ Confidence: Why not me?
  - ▸ Vulnerability: You're willing to try … And even fail
- Final thoughts

The Mental Game Behind Teaching

This module is here to make sure you avoid burnout. From our experience, it's unfair to ask people to go, go, go and do, do, do without giving them time to recharge. You've just done *a lot* of hard work. Now that you've spent so much time and energy investing in your project and working with others, it's time to give yourself a little pampering.

The following activities are all about self-care and providing you with ideas and strategies that promote your well-being. We know this isn't the end of the journey for you. As you continue to teach, to problem-solve, to innovate, and to lead, you'll need to spend time nurturing your own mental stamina. We encourage you to take care of yourself so you stay fresh and energized.

Use this module to invest in self-love. Based on our work with teachers, we've highlighted the areas that seem to greatly impact morale, and we've created activities to prevent burnout. As with the other modules in this book, use the parts that apply to *you*. We hope these ideas can help you tap into your strengths and give you the opportunity to recharge.

We invite you to come back to this section time and again, especially during the low points, so you can build yourself back up and stay empowered throughout your career. (For a full assessment of your teacher burnout level and how to get and stay out of burnout so you can keep your passion for teaching alive, see Amber Harper's book *Hacking Teacher Burnout*, also published by Times 10 Publications.)

Our Story Behind Self-Care: The Importance of Preventing Burnout

We're not embarrassed to admit we were a bit naive when we got into the whole innovation space. As excited as we were for the opportunity to lead innovation workshops for teachers (we hadn't yet developed the Startup methodology), we quickly learned that not everyone was ready to hit the ground running. Not all teachers were chomping at the bit to turn their ideas into action. In fact, we found that many teachers were flat-out exhausted by the thought of innovating, and rightfully so.

Teachers were skeptical of the innovation process, not for want of amazing ideas, but because they simply didn't have the energy to get hurt—again. After years of slowly being stripped of their autonomy, sitting through PD that wasn't helpful, and generally having their ideas rejected, the mere suggestion of receiving professional development hours for working on their own ideas for the classroom sounded too good to be true. Suspicious that we might represent yet another educational fad—they have a history of broken promises—we quickly understood why they didn't want to rush in.

For us, it was clear: Society and bad experiences had warped the mindsets of many teachers. They had become convinced they were "just teachers"; that they didn't know what they were talking about and were powerless and incapable. We understood that in order to prove just how wrong society was, we needed to give teachers a chance to prove just how incredible and capable they were, and how much their students needed them. This would require building up their mental stamina, because unfortunately in education—innovation seems to be an uphill battle.

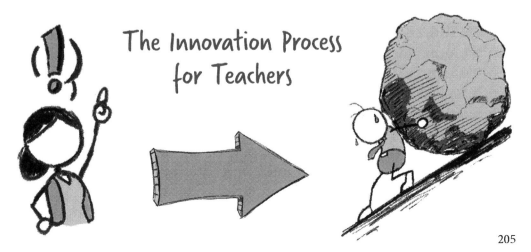

The Innovation Process for Teachers

As educators, we often have great ideas for how to improve teaching and learning, but let's face it: the odds are often stacked against us. It's hard to *do* something with those ideas, particularly if you have largely experienced setbacks and disappointments. It's hard to get the momentum you need to turn your ideas into projects when you feel overwhelmed, unsupported, or undervalued—and it's easy to frequently feel those emotions in education.

As we worked with teachers around the country, we began to ask ourselves: Why are some teachers more open to the idea of innovation than others? What causes the resistance we sometimes feel? What motivates some to run while others are wary of taking the first step? Why are some willing to look past the disappointments they'd experienced and try again, while others aren't?

We determined that a lot of it came down to a teacher's attitude. Did they still believe they had the power to create change, or had that belief been stripped from them? When we asked teachers, most said they went into teaching because they wanted to make a difference and impact lives. So what was happening to cause teachers to lose that can-do attitude they started out with?

And then it clicked. If we expected teachers to innovate, we needed to give them a space, an outlet where they could recharge. Years of rejection and heartbreak, years of being told no, years of training and development that treated them like robotic blobs incapable of original thought had drained their initial teaching optimism and shifted how they viewed their role, their capacity, and even themselves.

> "Teaching may be the only profession where you are required to get an advanced degree, including a rigorous internship, only to be treated like you have no idea what you're doing ... it's ironic. The act of removing teacher autonomy results in dampening our effectiveness."
> – Steven Singer, National Board Certified Teacher and Education Blogger

It's hard to do something with your ideas if you have experienced setbacks and disappointments. It's hard to find the energy to start—let alone finish—a new idea if you're constantly being told no. As educators, we often get told no. It may not be an outright no, but *no* takes on many forms. It's in how we're treated, how our role is defined, the amount of creative freedom we're given, the amount of responsibility, the amount of voice, and so on.

We can't tell you how many times we've heard an amazing idea from a teacher, only to have our enthusiastic "Let's do it!" followed by a "Yeah, but ..." Years of being told no have caused many teachers to feel disempowered. They often anticipate the no and stop before they even start. They want to protect themselves, to avoid investing time in an effort that may never materialize. Teachers get beaten down, and that wears away at our well-being, thus preventing us from reaching our full potential. (This is why we feel so many teachers leave.)

Since we know "no" is such a reality in the education space, we realized we needed to *do something* to help teachers prepare mentally so they have the endurance to deal with and overcome all of those "noes." Innovating is hard, but we're the ones responsible for giving students the educational experience they deserve, and it's up to us to elevate the profession to what we once believed it could be.

That's why we want to leave you with a space to build yourself up and remind yourself that you are an amazing leader and learning designer. Because once we stop believing in our own power to achieve and make a difference, once we grow too weary or tired, we stop achieving and making a difference. And we can't let that happen.

The Many Forms of

Administration

"We need to focus on _____ this year."

"Your job is to teach."

"We're putting our resources and budget toward X this year."

Excuses

"No one will support me/this idea."

"There's no time."

"There's no money."

"My administration won't go for this."

"I'll never get parents on board."

"It's not my content area."

"It's the parents. They just..."

"We've tried that already. Doesn't work."

"Yeah, but the students just won't..."

Doubts/Insecurities

"What if I lose my job?"
"I don't know enough."
"I'll just screw it up."
"My colleagues will think I'm trying to make them look bad."

The World

- You're JUST a teacher.
- That's not your job.
- Stop trying so hard; nothing's going to change.

Pressure

They won't say it, but you can FEEL it:

Parents
Family
Colleagues
The community

The Pretend Yes

"We really want to hear from you."
"We should do that..."
"We love innovation, just..."
"We can, after..."

The suggestion box rejection

Tap Into Your Strengths:
Recharge, Refresh, Repeat

While we're not going to pretend that we're experts on emotional intelligence (or social-emotional learning), we know that teaching comes with an abundance of emotional baggage. You've invested time and mental resources into your project and into your students. It's easy to get tired. Being a successful learning designer and Startup Teacher is part mental exercise. And as with any sort of exercise, the more we practice and train, the stronger we will become, and the more successful we'll become at elevating teaching and learning. It's a matter of taking the time to flex what you already naturally possess.

We previously mentioned the importance of attitude in the ability for teachers to innovate. So if attitude is everything, what shapes our attitude? What exactly is it that helps teachers to jump the hurdles and push through setbacks so they can move forward with their ideas? While leading our workshops, we began to notice similar attributes among the educators who, when given the opportunity to innovate, were ready to hit the ground running. These were the traits that helped nourish that positive attitude teachers need to get started with (and finish!) this work:

Heart: You care and are driven by your desire to make a difference.

Optimism: You believe change is possible and see the opportunity in situations.

Curiosity: You're a lifelong learner, open to new experiences.

Confidence: You believe in yourself and your ability to bring ideas to life.

Vulnerability: You're true to yourself in the face of societal pressure.

If you picked up this book, we know you are already a Startup Teacher and are confident that you possess these qualities. Now it's important that you take care of those qualities—as it's the secret to keeping your sanity and promoting your mental health.

Common Traits of a
STARTUP TEACHER

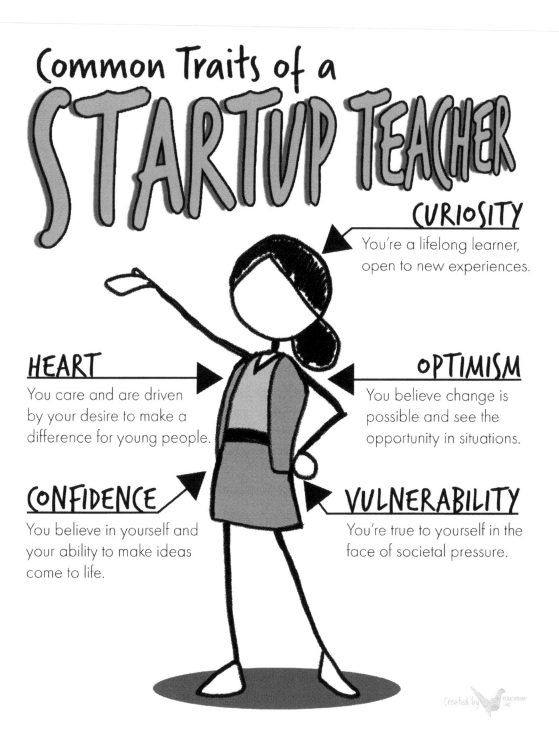

CURIOSITY
You're a lifelong learner, open to new experiences.

HEART
You care and are driven by your desire to make a difference for young people.

OPTIMISM
You believe change is possible and see the opportunity in situations.

CONFIDENCE
You believe in yourself and your ability to make ideas come to life.

VULNERABILITY
You're true to yourself in the face of societal pressure.

Created by EDUCATORS

Yes, there's overlap between the qualities. They feed off of and complement each other, making them hard to completely isolate.

	**When nurtured:** You reclaim your sense of joy and purpose. Students are at the center because they are at the heart of everything you do. **When ignored:** You lose your focus–your passion–and get mired in initiatives you don't believe in and caught up in activities that don't matter to you. Students' needs aren't met. You may stop caring.
	**When nurtured:** You know how to handle adversity. You're able to find the opportunities when presented with challenges. You know how to persevere and can push through setbacks, so you can keep going when the going gets tough. **When ignored:** You lose your belief that change is possible. You become disempowered and frustrated. You may get defensive or put up walls. You may stop trying.
	**When nurtured:** You seek out new skills. You're open to learning, exploring, and playing, because you want to continuously grow and improve as an educator (and human). **When ignored:** You only know what you know. You become closed-off and unapproachable. You stay in a rut.
	**When nurtured:** You're comfortable pushing yourself. You're not afraid to speak your mind. You're happy to take the lead on projects because if not you, who? **When ignored:** You lose your voice. You may feel neglected or think negatively about yourself and your capabilities. Your own self-doubts prevent you from growing.
	**When nurtured:** You strive to be your authentic self in the face of societal pressure. You live by your own standards, never aiming for perfection, but rather at being the best you can be. People are happy to approach you because you are unabashedly *you.* **When ignored:** You become too scared to take risks. You place too much emphasis on what others will think about you. You strive for a perfection that no one can attain. Caving to societal pressures leads to your unhappiness.

Through our work, we noticed that these qualities greatly shaped educators' views about themselves and their power to achieve. Nurturing these qualities enabled educators to draw strength and endurance to overcome obstacles. Inversely, we also noticed that when these qualities were neglected, the result was debilitating to teachers' abilities to achieve.

That's why we've included this series of activities to help you nurture your strengths. Taking care of yourself means spending time on your emotional health. When you feel tired or drained, remember how incredible you are and find constructive ways to build yourself back up. We created this section to give you the chance to clear out the mental clutter, shed the baggage, and recharge.

We invite you to train for the mental game that is teaching. Take a moment to ignore the constant emails and demands and focus a little on you (you have our permission). You don't have to complete every task, nor do you have to proceed in order. Skip around and connect to what you feel you need right now. Nurturing your strengths will give you the mental stamina you need to dive deeper into your work and perform to the best of your abilities.

> Your students will certainly benefit from you exploring these traits, but feel free to also explore these traits *with* your students! Make copies of any activities and use them with your classes as you see fit.

Use the activities in this section personally and professionally, solo or with a group, with your colleagues or with your students. This is a time for self-reflection, healing, and remembering that you have more voice and control in your classroom than you might feel. We hope that it will rekindle your joy of teaching, remind you of your passions, and help you recall all it is that *you* have to offer.

Remember: What you do is amazing. You make a difference, and you have the power to make things happen. We need more teachers like you to stay in the classroom, so please take care of yourself and remember how much students need good teachers like *you*.

Strengths-Training: Your strengths need exercise!

In the same way athletes train, we invite you to train. What you do is so important, much more important than any sporting event. Focusing on your mental health allows you to be proactive and leverage your strengths so you can clear those hurdles smoothly, with less stress and burnout. Just like an athlete, we don't expect you to take the journey alone. When athletes get tired, coaches and teammates cheer them on and help them tap into that inner voice to keep going. Find the "coaches and teammates" who can support you. Surround yourself with those who will encourage you, act as your cheerleaders, and push you through (especially when the going gets tough).

Warm-Up. Start small. Take time for self-reflection. Understand who you are and what you're about so you can focus on initiatives that matter most. Use this next section to remind yourself of your strengths and what you have to offer.

Strengthen-Up. Build on your strengths and practice using them. Shed initiatives that don't add value. Use this next section to flex the strengths you already have and turn those qualities you've let get flabby back into muscle.

Find Your "Workout" Buds. Find like-minded folks who are headed in the same direction. Be authentic about what is important to *you*. The half-assed "yes" will fizzle fast, so find people who are truly on the same page as you. See if you can find a partner to engage in this process with you.

Dig Deep and Push Each Other. Once you find your people, push each other to keep moving toward your goal. When you're doing something hard, it's easy to get exhausted and find excuses to quit. Mental exhaustion is part of teaching, but when you're surrounded by support, you're more likely to keep going. Have a personal "coach" to keep you accountable. As you continue on your journey, lean on each other for encouragement to push through.

Succeed. Feel that endorphin rush! Enjoy the sense of satisfaction as you complete tasks and accomplish goals. Know that you made a tremendous impact, and investing in this work can reap amazing results.

Activities to Focus on Self-Care

You've reached the most interactive part of this module. This is where you will work on five key qualities of self-care and choose the activities and ideas that best serve you. You'll find the qualities on the following pages:

Heart

What do I care about?
Why am I doing this?

Definition: You care. You want what's best for your students. It's not just a job; you're driven by your desire to make an impact. Kids are not numbers. Heart helps you understand your purpose and be intentional about what you choose to do. Consider it your North Star, your guide when it comes to choosing what to work on and why.

> Heart is the motivating factor for what you do. When you no longer believe in what you're doing, when it doesn't feel "right," you lose your sense of purpose.

Working on HEART helps you:

- Remember how incredible you are.

- Remember what you love.

- Reconnect with what you love.

- Remember why you became a teacher.

- Remember what matters to *you* as an educator.

Are you feeling…	Signs you may need to devote time to HEART.
Disengaged	Are you passively watching (or zoning out altogether) rather than engaging in activities?
Taken for granted	Starting to think you don't matter? Does it feel like people dump on you and expect you to clean up after them?
Unsatisfied	Do you find yourself wondering why you're doing what you do?

Activity #1: Remember How Incredible You Are

In the hustle and bustle of life and teaching, it's easy to swallow and internalize all the negatives we hear (and all too often say to ourselves). We wouldn't let a student or a friend get mired in faults; you owe it to yourself not to, either.

Paint a Portrait: What Makes You, *You*?

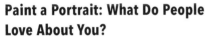

Remember how special you are. Write down what makes you unique: those qualities that make you stand out from the crowd. There's only one you. Appreciate it.

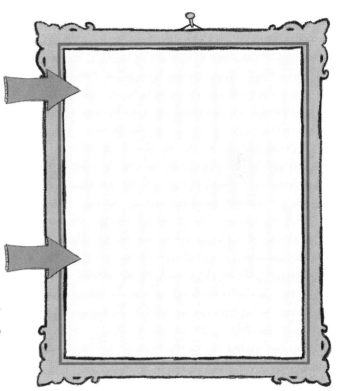

Paint a Portrait: What Do People Love About You?

It's usually easier for others to pick up on our strengths and qualities. Pick a few people, anyone who really knows you, and ask them to describe their favorite thing about you. Write them down. Come back to this list when you need a reminder of how great you are.

Create a "You're Awesome" Folder

1. Save positive artifacts from parents, students, peers, and others (notes, drawings, emails).

2. Put them in a folder.

3. Take them out any time you feel like you're not enough, and remember that other people clearly think you are.

*Thank you for this idea, Debbie Jones!

Activity #2: Remember What You Love

Your identity is not your profession; you're so much more than that. Don't lose who you are. Staying true to yourself and recognizing how to nurture your well-being will keep you happier and more satisfied in all aspects of your life. Use these activities to remember what you value, and rekindle those aspects of your life that bring you joy.

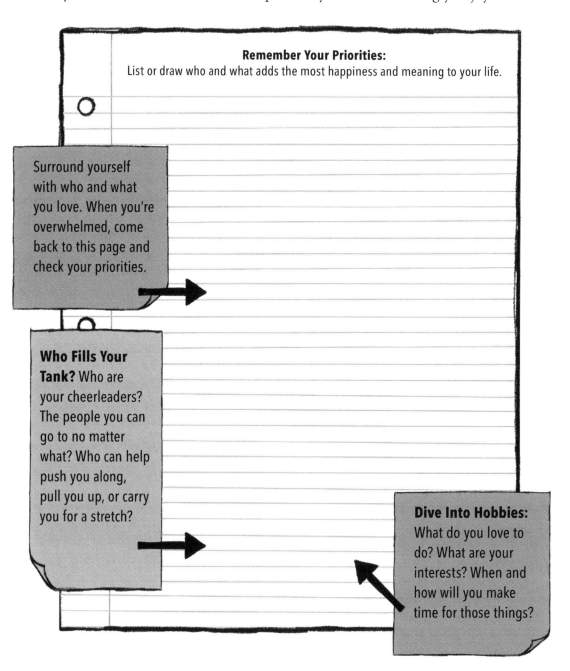

Remember Your Priorities:
List or draw who and what adds the most happiness and meaning to your life.

Surround yourself with who and what you love. When you're overwhelmed, come back to this page and check your priorities.

Who Fills Your Tank? Who are your cheerleaders? The people you can go to no matter what? Who can help push you along, pull you up, or carry you for a stretch?

Dive Into Hobbies: What do you love to do? What are your interests? When and how will you make time for those things?

Activity #3: Reconnect with What You Love

Be intentional with how you spend your time and who you spend your time with. Use these activities to strategize how you can create outlets of time to reconnect with what you love.

Take time to nurture your relationships.

We all need human connection. Make yourself present and create a plan to reach out. Being intentional about spending time with those you love and value–those who fill your tank–will ensure you get the chance to nurture those relationships.

- Say hi.
- Send a note.
- Stop by.
- Plan an outing.

You get what you give!

Ditch the Distractions

If you want to be less busy and prioritize what matters to you, try to free yourself from those activities that don't add as much value to your life. List your time distractors (e.g., social media, binge watching, online shopping, gaming).

Strategize: How might you redirect this time toward a priority that gives you a deeper sense of joy?

Tip: Stop saying *yes* to everything!

You don't have to say "yes" to every ask. At times, we all do things we don't love because A) that's life and B) someone has to do it, but we often take on more than necessary.

Brainstorm: What can you *stop* doing?

What initiatives or activities can you get rid of?

Activity #4: Remember Why You Became a Teacher

Too often, we've seen teachers who are pressured to focus on a responsibility that doesn't align with their purpose *(cough cough, test scores)*. Taking time to remember why you're doing all this—your purpose—will help you craft a vision for your work and better define your goals for you and your students.

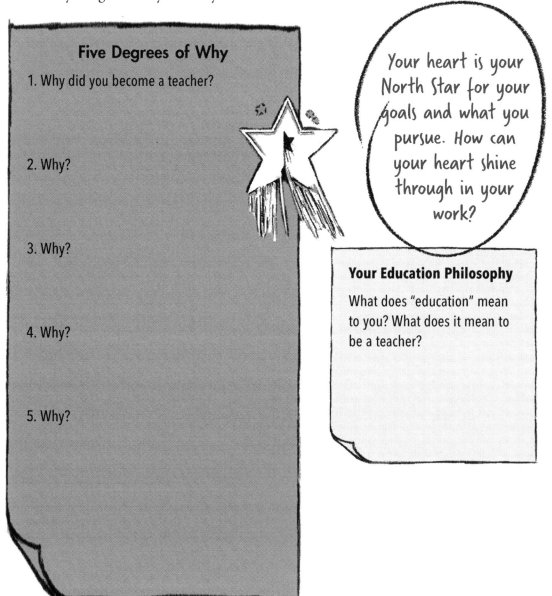

Five Degrees of Why

1. Why did you become a teacher?

2. Why?

3. Why?

4. Why?

5. Why?

Your heart is your North Star for your goals and what you pursue. How can your heart shine through in your work?

Your Education Philosophy

What does "education" mean to you? What does it mean to be a teacher?

Activity #5: Remember What Matters to *you* as an educator

Clearly articulating your goals will help you refine your efforts and focus your energy, ultimately leading to your desired impact.

What are your goals as an educator? What kind of impact do you want to make?		
Short-term: (in the next month)	**Reflect:** What are you doing to achieve this goal?	**Reflect:** What *could* you do?
Long-term: (the school year)	**Reflect:** What are you doing to achieve this goal?	**Reflect:** What *could* you do?
Career: What kind of legacy do you want to leave for your students? What do you want to be remembered for?	**Reflect:** What are you doing to achieve this goal?	**Reflect:** What *could* you do?

Heart is the foundation of everything else. Trust your heart. Nurture it. Follow it.

optimism

Yes! Change is possible.

Definition: You believe change is possible. You look for opportunities to make things better. You assume the best—in others and in situations. You believe in the abilities of others. Optimism will help you push through when times get tough; it helps you handle adversity. Along with heart, it's your motivator, your energizer. If you no longer believe something can be changed, you're more likely to give up.

> Optimism is not to be confused with being happy all the time; rather, it's about maintaining a positive outlook on life.

Working on OPTIMISM helps you:

- Reenergize.
- Stay positive by finding the opportunity in all situations.
- Coach yourself through adversity.
- Influence others' attitudes in a positive way.

Are you feeling…	Signs you may need to cultivate OPTIMISM.
Negative	Do you find yourself complaining or venting without seeking solutions or letting go?
Jaded	Are you feeling like nothing you do matters?
Exhausted	Do you feel overwhelmed, like you have too much on your plate?

Activity #1: Reenergize

Before you can help make life better for others, you need to make life better for *you*. Use these activities to help you refuel.

Basic Needs Inventory

Even the most optimistic person will crumble if their basic needs aren't met. Are you taking care of yourself?

1. Are you getting enough:
   - nutritious food?
   - sleep?
   - exercise?

2. Are you making time for:
   - yourself?
   - sunshine/nature?
   - the people you love?

If you answered *no* to any of these questions, it's time to *recharge*!

You are not selfish if you keep some of your time for yourself. You give yourself and your time to others ALL. THE. TIME. *Keeping* some of your own time for yourself will only help you better serve others.

Recharging Station: Invest in Me Time

Take a nap, take the day off, do something fun to blow off steam. What are your favorite, most-effective ways to relieve stress, unwind, reconnect, or refocus? Draw, list, or journal what *you* need.

***Any time you're feeling overwhelmed, come back to this list!

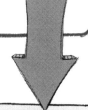

Activity #2: Stay Positive by Finding the Opportunity in All Situations

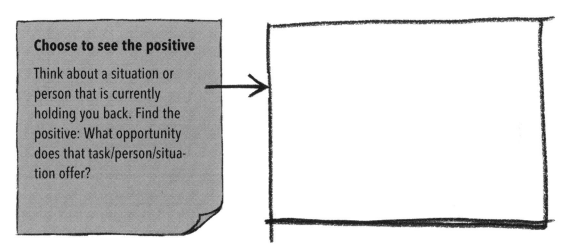

Optimism can keep you focused on the positive while processing out the negative in healthy, productive ways. This does not mean you ignore problems or blindly skip through life. It means you don't just vent, you reinvent by finding what you can control and making the most of every situation.

Choose to see the positive

Think about a situation or person that is currently holding you back. Find the positive: What opportunity does that task/person/situation offer?

When frustrations pile up, remember to focus on what you can control. Sometimes it's the little things, like how you choose to react. Sometimes it's how you respond (or don't respond). Use the next few pages to help turn a few current frustrations into possible opportunities. See if you can find the positives in the frustrations.

Seizing frustrations: what can you control?

List five current frustrations:

1.

2.

3.

4.

5.

What can you *learn* from that frustration?
What opportunity might exist in it?

1.

2.

3.

4.

5.

What's one thing you can do about this?

1.

2.

3.

4.

5.

Take action! What happened?

1.

2.

3.

4.

5.

Activity #3: Coach Yourself Through Adversity

Develop optimism so you can coach yourself (and others) to manage frustrations and failures. This will help you understand when to proceed and when to back away.

Managing "Failure"

What does failure mean to you?

What do you say to students/colleagues when they don't immediately succeed with something? Do you apply that same advice to yourself?

When you feel like you've failed, what do you normally do to boost yourself back up?

Even the most optimistic person needs a cheerleader from time to time. Who has your back? Who can help hold you up when you stumble? Who can you trust to tell you what you need to hear?

Learning From Mistakes to Move Forward

Look at each column. When something doesn't go right, how do you know when to employ each of these coping strategies?	Manage Emotions	Regroup and Start Fresh	Revise and Retry	Let Go
Personally				
Professionally				

Activity #4: Influence the Attitude of Others in a Positive Way

Optimism grows optimism. By focusing on the good and choosing gratitude, you can spread optimism and make your life—and everyone else's—easier.

Gratitude List

Think about your classroom, school, and community. For each, list what makes you thankful:

In your life:

Students:

Colleagues:

Parents:

Administration:

Wider Community:

Building people up helps build a culture of positivity and nurtures self-confidence. As you note your gratitudes, find a way to share them with others.

The benefits of gratitude are well-researched. For more gratitude activities, go to Module Three and also check out the resources at the Greater Good Science Center.

Who or what makes you believe change is *possible*?

Hold tight to these things and people!

Being positive—optimistic—won't guarantee you success, but being negative will guarantee failure. You control yourself and how you react; choosing to see the opportunity in every situation will help you identify where you can make an impact.

Curiosity
You're a lifelong learner.

Definition: You're a lifelong learner. You seek knowledge, ideas, and solutions. You ask lots of good, probing questions. You enjoy tinkering and playing with new tools and ideas. Curiosity will help you not only develop great ideas but learn from others and be resourceful in using what you have.

> Curiosity is vital for keeping ourselves engaged, informed, and excited about our life, our work, and our world.

Working on CURIOSITY helps you:

- Keep learning.

- Devote time to play.

- Develop flexible thinking.

Are you feeling...	Signs you may need more CURIOSITY in your life.
Disinterested	Do you shy away from things you're usually interested in?
Bored	Stuck in a rut? Going through the motions?
Complacent	Due to time or a busy schedule, have you stopped seeking out new ideas and experiences?

Activity #1: Keep Learning

Accept and enjoy new challenges. Keep life interesting, even exciting, as you seek out adventures in learning. Be open to new experiences, explore new ideas, learn new things in new ways.

They say the older you get, the fewer questions you ask. Write down at least five questions you have about the world around you.

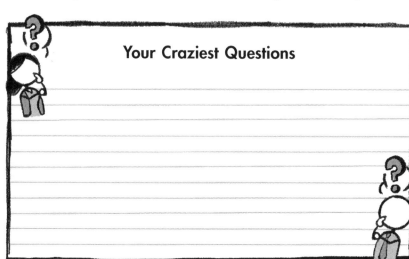

Your Craziest Questions

Engage in a conversation with someone you don't know.	Take time to think. Let your mind wander and see where it goes.	Think of a place you've always wanted to visit, and go there (virtually counts!).
Try a new recipe or order a new food.	Ask deep questions of a person you care about.	Experience something new.
Ask students for their favorite thing to do or play right now, and give it a shot.	Ask someone in your life to show or teach you how to do something they love.	Talk to someone who holds an opposing opinion about an issue, and listen to their why.

Play Curiosity Tic-Tac-Toe

Activity #2: Devote Time to Play

Children learn through play. Get back to your developmental roots to get your hands dirty. To do this, make sure you devote time for play. Free time is essential to your well-being and to stay curious.

What are two things you want to learn? When will you do it?	What are two things you want to try? When will you do it?	What are two topics you want to dig deeper into? When will you do it?

Put down your phone, turn off the TV/radio/computer, and find fifteen to thirty minutes to just BE. Alone.

What happened?
Where did your mind wander?

A Note About Free Time:

Free time is any use of time for personal enjoyment and pleasure, including, but not limited to, personal time, detox time, thinking time, family time, and play time. Maintaining work/life balance seems to be even harder as a teacher because we want to give our all. Staying curious–sure, about teaching but also about life–will help rejuvenate ourselves and better connect us with everyone in our lives, including our students.

So...

When will you set aside time to:

Ask questions:

Play:

Explore:

Do nothing:

Let your mind wander:

Activity #3: Develop Flexible Thinking

Developing your professional curiosity helps you increase both flexible thinking and potential resources. You don't know what you don't know until you start looking, listening, and trying new things. Home in on your colleagues, your building, and your greater PLN.

List two or more colleagues who teach in a completely different style than you. Ask them to help you try a new way. When will you do it?	List two or more people you know who can show/teach/explain something new to you. When will you do it?	List two+ authors, bloggers, YouTubers, or podcasters you'd like to check out. When will you DO it?

Try a:	What:	When:	Your takeaways:
New book:			
Conference:			
Twitter chat:			
Edcamp:			
New tech tool:			
Ed podcast:			
Other:			

Staying curious is the only way to ensure you continue to grow. Don't settle! For your own excitement and enjoyment and for the good of your students, keep curiosity alive. Fight resistance. Be open. Keep life interesting, even exciting, as you seek adventures in learning.

Confidence

Why not me?

Definition: You believe you can make your ideas happen. You know that if you don't take it upon yourself to do something, no one else will. Confidence helps you take charge of your ideas.

Working on CONFIDENCE helps you:

NOT to be confused with arrogance!

- Know your strengths.
- Face your fears.
- Build resilience.
- Speak up.

Are you feeling...	Signs you need to work on CONFIDENCE.
Defensive	Do you have your guard up or find you're intimidated by people?
Suspicious	Do you feel like everyone is out to get you?
Hesitant	Do "what ifs" hold you back?

Activity #1: Know Your Strengths

Do you believe in yourself? Take stock of all the big and little things that make you *you*. All that you bring to the table. To serve others, you need to know what you have to give others.

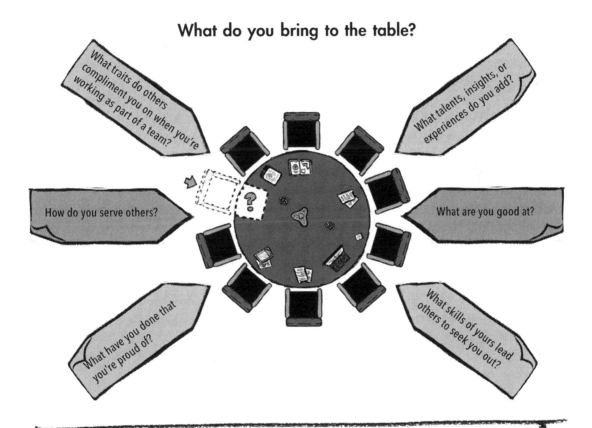

What do you bring to the table?

- What traits do others compliment you on when you're working as part of a team?
- What talents, insights, or experiences do you add?
- How do you serve others?
- What are you good at?
- What have you done that you're proud of?
- What skills of yours lead others to seek you out?

Strengths Check

Remember when you were a kid, and people asked what you were good at? You likely thought they meant things: baseball, swimming, drawing. As adults, we learn that most strengths are more intangible and hold more value (e.g., patience, kindness, perseverance). When we say strengths, we're talking about all those underlying skills, traits, and abilities that make you *you*.

Activity #2: Face Your Fears

What scares you? Examine your fears, then slow down and think through what might happen if you were to put yourself out there. Usually, it's nothing. We let our fears and insecurities get in the way of taking action. Take small steps to boost your confidence and put yourself out there.

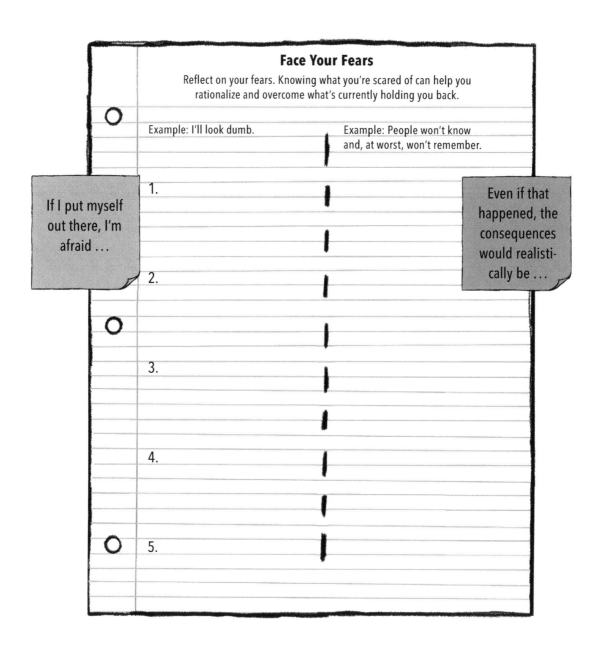

Activity #3: Build Resilience

For any project, it's vital to separate the project from yourself. It's not personal if something doesn't work. Feedback—even criticism—is one of the best ways to improve your practice. Stay confident and let feedback inform you, not deflate you.

It's hard not to take criticism personally. Train your brain to hear criticism, even from the harshest critics, as opportunities to learn, improve, and grow.

Feedback Filter

When people say ...	They are really trying to say ...	So I will use that feedback to ...
That's stupid.	I don't understand why this is important.	Clarify my *why* so I can explain it to others.
That's fine but I really think you should ...		
Wow, that sounds like a *lot*.		
You won't be able to make that work.		

Confidence Boosters to Bounce Back:

Even the most resilient among us needs a pep talk from time to time. Use your own confidence to help you spring back when you're feeling deflated.

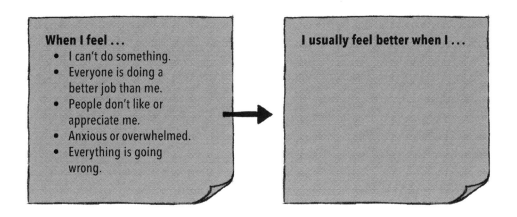

When I feel ...
- I can't do something.
- Everyone is doing a better job than me.
- People don't like or appreciate me.
- Anxious or overwhelmed.
- Everything is going wrong.

I usually feel better when I ...

Activity #4: Speak Up!

Don't be afraid to speak up and stand up. Education is overrun by petty initiatives, sometimes because we succumb to those who speak the loudest (even if their ideas stink). You have nothing to lose by trying. Stand up for what matters to you the most.

Speak Up Strategy

Confidence allows you to reflect honestly about your strengths and weaknesses. Since speaking up is so important when it comes to solving problems, ask yourself these questions when you have something to say:

1. Is this worth speaking out on?

2. Do you know when, where, and how to present your ideas so others are more receptive?

3. Do you understand *who* needs to hear *what*? And the best time or method to deliver your message?

4. Are you being strategic in what and how much you share? People may start filtering you out if you're always sharing.

Why Not Me?

Think of all that you have seen and heard about in education: all the initiatives, books, blogs, and resources. What's the most ridiculous idea you've been forced to support or implement?

What should have been done?

Did you speak up? Why or why not?

Remember, your voice counts! *You* have good ideas, so don't be afraid to make them known.

The Fallacy of the Overachiever

Do you feel like you're annoying people when you tell them your ideas?

Do people make you feel bad or guilty when you tell them about a project?

Do you feel like you have to lie low with ideas you're working on?

Ever had the weird criticism "overachiever" thrown in your face? You're not an over-achiever; you're a **damn good teacher!** Having the confidence to take action is a good quality.

Don't let the insecurities of others stop you.

It is common to have moments of doubt, to question yourself and worry about whether you're doing the right thing the right way. That's okay. That's your heart making sure you're staying true to your mission. Just don't stop. Believe in yourself and believe in your ideas.

If not you, who?

If not now, when?

Vulnerability

You're willing to try ... and even fail.

Definition: You're willing to put yourself out there and get out of your comfort zone to achieve your vision of success. You can accept some levels of uncertainty as you strive for growth, not perfection. You understand you must open yourself up emotionally in order to grow both personally and professionally.

> Vulnerability is about being true to yourself in the face of societal pressure.

Working on **VULNERABILITY** helps you:

- Open yourself to others.

- Define success in your terms.

- Let go of toxic habits.

Are you feeling...	Signs you could be more VULNERABLE.
Judged	Do you feel like everyone is talking about you? Are you constantly worried about what other people think?
Pressured	Do you do things because (you feel) they're expected? Do you do things because they're what others want, or what you want?
Inauthentic	Are you using energy to pretend to be what you are not?

Activity #1: Open Yourself to Others

Tear down the walls and open yourself to others. Being vulnerable doesn't mean you give everything to everyone, but it does mean you allow others to see the real you. To achieve what matters to you the most, let go of insecurities and stop worrying about what others will think. What matters is what *you* think.

Watch or read Brené Brown, who explains the value of vulnerability.

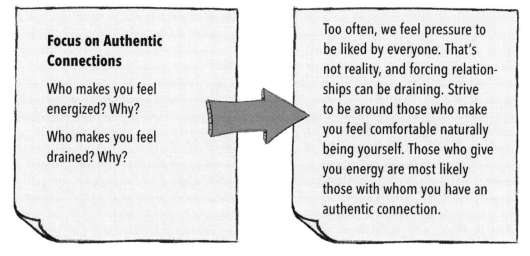

Focus on Authentic Connections

Who makes you feel energized? Why?

Who makes you feel drained? Why?

Too often, we feel pressure to be liked by everyone. That's not reality, and forcing relationships can be draining. Strive to be around those who make you feel comfortable naturally being yourself. Those who give you energy are most likely those with whom you have an authentic connection.

Even the most confident person usually has an aspect of themselves they don't like and that they keep under wraps. List those things you don't want people to see or learn about you. Then, reflect on whether keeping them hidden is truly serving you.

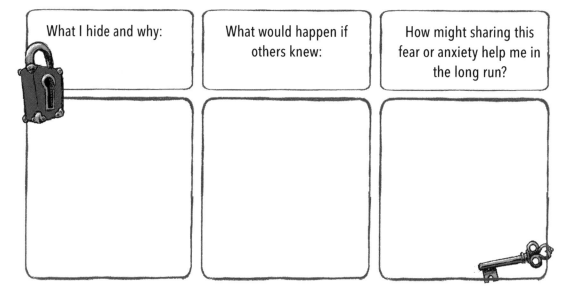

What I hide and why:

What would happen if others knew:

How might sharing this fear or anxiety help me in the long run?

Activity #2: Define Success in Your Terms

Failure is okay. If you want to make any project successful, if you want to be happy, you must let go of everyone else's idea of perfection and success, and live life by *your* standards.

SUCCESS

How do you think society defines it?

How do you define it for yourself?

How do you define it for your classroom or students?

Define it so it doesn't define you!

Reflect: Are you working to achieve society's definitions or your own?

Grow: What steps can you take to work toward living by your definition?

PERFECTION

How do you think society defines it?

How do you define it for yourself?

How do you define it for your classroom or students?

Aim for growth, not perfection.

245

Activity #3: Let Go of Toxic Habits

Sometimes we're our own worst enemy. We spend too much time and energy beating ourselves up, instead of recognizing how amazing we are. Get out of your own way, and you'll be a lot happier in the long run.

Take the weight off.

Each of the toxic habits on this page can put a strain on our mental stamina and prevent us from being true to ourselves. They can make us feel heavy or fake. If you see this activity in yourself, recognize it and try your best to *let go*. Trust us. It'll feel amazing to take that weight off your shoulders:

Stop doubting yourself.

Believe in your ideas. Explore them. If you don't do them, no one else will. Don't let toxic people hold power over you. Know your value and treat yourself with all the self-worth you can muster.

We've noticed one major strategy to overcome *any* of these setbacks: taking a social media break.

Stop taking everything personally.

Nothing is wrong with you if an idea flops or plans don't go smoothly. Recognize feedback and failures as opportunities to learn and grow.

Stop comparing yourself.

If you're doing your best and being your best, then you're doing an amazing job. Life is not a competition. It's about living the life *you* define and being happy with it.

Stop trying to fit in.

Part of being vulnerable is being honest with yourself. Your thoughts, your interests, and your opinions are what make you, *you*. If a person doesn't like them, then maybe that person (or group) wasn't the right fit for you. Or maybe you need to work on yourself and how you come across to others.

Stop worrying what others think.

You will never please everyone (no one does), so stop trying. If you're doing what you feel is right, in a spirit of kindness and positivity, that's all you can do.

We need to stop worrying about what others think. It's so simple to say, yet so much harder to do. Vulnerability is perhaps the hardest trait to nurture and model for others because it exposes so much of who we are. Your work will benefit from this practice. Your students will benefit from this practice. Your relationships will benefit from this practice. *You* will benefit from this practice. Take a deep breath and take one step at a time. You've got this.

Final Thoughts:

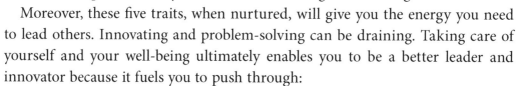

Teaching is an exhausting (and exhilarating) profession. Add to that all the daily demands put on us and it's easy to see why burnout is so common. We hope these activities help you feel revived and refreshed. Use them, adapt them, share them—with colleagues, students, or your community—and help flex your social-emotional muscles and further hone your natural Startup Teacher inclinations. When you do, you'll be better positioned to use the Educator Canvas to tackle challenges and solve the problems so you can elevate teaching and learning.

Moreover, these five traits, when nurtured, will give you the energy you need to lead others. Innovating and problem-solving can be draining. Taking care of yourself and your well-being ultimately enables you to be a better leader and innovator because it fuels you to push through:

Quality	Natural Inclination	When Developed	Benefits	Impact
Heart	You do things for the right reasons: students!	Your purpose is meaningful and clear to others.	You're excited about what you do, and others are excited with you.	Increased joy, outcomes, and connection for you and your students
Heart, Leadership & the Canvas:	HEART helps you prioritize initiatives and share your purpose and vision clearly. Guided by heart, you don't waste time on what's not important. When people understand the value behind what you're doing, they're more likely to jump on board.			
Optimism	You keep going; you know that anything is possible with effort.	You're able to overcome any obstacle that lands in your path.	You become more resilient because you can see the opportunities in all situations.	You're able to reduce stress and burnout because you see the good in everything.
Optimism, Leadership & the Canvas:	OPTIMISM helps you persevere because you believe in what you're doing and know that any outcome is a step toward discovering a solution. You motivate and energize others. Your belief, not only in the idea but in the team, makes you a great leader.			

Curiosity	You want to learn more about many things.	You seek out answers wherever they may be, even if they conflict with your original ideas.	You have the natural capacity to try new things and the resources to solve problems.	You're more likely to find the best solution for any problem, stay energized, and want to do more.
Curiosity, Leadership & the Canvas:	CURIOSITY ensures you welcome the chance to learn with and from others *and* look for new ways to learn. Your desire to remain curious breeds curiosity, sparking innovation everywhere you go.			
Confidence	You're confident in your ideas and take on initiatives, because if not you, then who?	You believe in your ability to make things happen and naturally lead others to work with you.	You can build support for ideas and use every resource to its maximum potential.	You're more likely to succeed in what you do because you believe in yourself and those around you.
Confidence, Leadership & the Canvas:	CONFIDENCE helps you be proactive with your ideas because you believe in them and yourself. Your authenticity and conviction, coupled with your passion, allow you to be convincing with your words and actions, helping you to lead others in your work.			
Vulnerability	You define success on your own terms and intentionally work to achieve that success.	You're able to resist the pressures of others and be true to yourself.	You're able to lead an authentic life and work on what you believe in.	You're able to attain the success you seek and continuously grow as a person.
Vulnerability, Leadership & the Canvas:	VULNERABILITY pushes you to act because you believe it's right, even if that makes you the black sheep. Since you know yourself and know where you need help, you can let go of the need for control, and trust others to contribute and take ownership of your ideas, expanding your impact.			

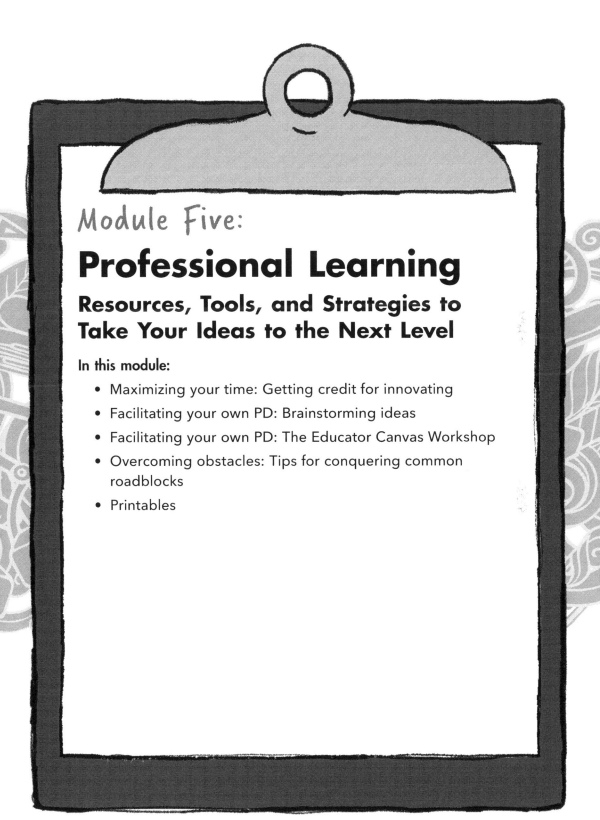

Module Five:

Professional Learning

Resources, Tools, and Strategies to Take Your Ideas to the Next Level

In this module:

- Maximizing your time: Getting credit for innovating
- Facilitating your own PD: Brainstorming ideas
- Facilitating your own PD: The Educator Canvas Workshop
- Overcoming obstacles: Tips for conquering common roadblocks
- Printables

 This resources section is completely plug and play and not meant to be read straight through. Much of this book is modular and designed for you to skip around. Scan through the tools and find those that fit your needs.

Welcome to Section Five! Being a Startup Teacher is about enabling education to adapt and evolve to changing times nimbly and quickly, and many moving pieces can help facilitate that process. As we've stated before, the problem-solving and innovation process is hardly ever as straightforward as we'd like to imagine. No two situations are alike, and every journey starts and ends at different places.

As such, we've designed a variety of tools, deep dives, and resources to make your journey easier as you improve education and revamp your professional development space. As always, adapt and use these tools as you see fit.

Share Your Work!

Use the hashtag #StartupTeacher, and share what you're working on. We can't wait to see what you're doing.

Maximizing Your Time: Getting Credit for Innovating

Too often we only get professional learning or recertification credit for sitting at a workshop (seat hours)—even if we have accomplished nothing. As outlined in our introduction, we want more valuable professional learning time to help educators like you solve the challenges you face in the classroom.

If you love that idea, too, use the following resources to make your case for getting credit for completing the Canvas and implementing your solutions.

Make the Case

Need to "justify" this work as PD? Professional learning can look different and be effective. We set out to design the PD we craved as teachers. But beyond our thoughts about what makes good PD, *The Startup Teacher Playbook* and the Educator Canvas exemplify the Four Prerequisites for Effective Professional Learning, as well as the Standards for Professional Learning as defined by Learning Forward.

Four Prerequisites for Effective Professional Learning	
Educators' commitment to students, all students, is the foundation of effective professional learning.	The project management tools in *The Startup Teacher Playbook* are designed to spark problem-solving and innovation with and for *students*. Educators working through the Canvas are dedicated to finding solutions to better ensure *all* students have the best learning experiences possible.
Each educator involved in professional learning comes to the experience ready to learn.	When teachers are excited about and interested in the topic and are able to work on things about which they are passionate, they are always ready. Moreover, when teachers are supported in that work, they come to the experience with excitement and energy.
Because there are disparate experience levels and use of practice among educators, professional learning can foster collaborative inquiry and learning that enhances individual and collective performance.	*The Startup Teacher Playbook* tools, specifically the Educator Canvas, work for teachers with any level of experience. They foster collaborative inquiry, even if teachers work on projects solo, as they seek ideas and feedback from others. The tools are also designed for both solo and group work.
Like all learners, educators learn in different ways and at different rates.	The self-paced nature of *The Startup Teacher Playbook* allows educators to work at their own pace and tackle challenges that help them grow incrementally. Because it's a process for problem-solving and project management, educators grow skills through the work, enhancing their abilities no matter where they start.

Learning Forward Standards for Professional Learning	The Startup Teacher Playbook and the Educator Canvas
LEARNING COMMUNITIES: Professional learning that increases educator effectiveness and results for all students occurs within learning communities committed to continuous improvement, collective responsibility, and goal alignment.	The Startup Teacher Playbook process and the Educator Canvas emphasize the importance of peer collaboration while providing a framework to support such work. This allows educators to learn and grow together while creating learning environments more desirable and productive for students.
LEADERSHIP: Professional learning that increases educator effectiveness and results for all students requires skillful leaders who develop capacity, advocate, and create support systems for professional learning.	Designed to cultivate the leadership capacity in *all* educators, *The Startup Teacher Playbook* process provides a clear support system for teachers to advocate for change. Everyone benefits when teachers are encouraged to grow and see themselves as leaders.
RESOURCES: Professional learning that increases educator effectiveness and results for all students requires prioritizing, monitoring, and coordinating resources for educator learning.	The resources within *The Startup Teacher Playbook* provide all the brainstorming, project planning, and designing resources needed in an easy-to-copy format (download the Educator Canvas at theeducatorslab.com). Why not grow that skill in *all* teachers?
DATA: Professional learning that increases educator effectiveness and results for all students uses a variety of sources and types of student, educator, and system data to plan, assess, and evaluate professional learning.	*The Startup Teacher Playbook* process is designed to have clear outcomes: teachers will work to improve themselves and their classrooms by engaging in reflection, research, and project management. Even if a project "fails," an educator will walk away with positive data about their personal growth.
LEARNING DESIGNS: Professional learning that increases educator effectiveness and results for all students integrates theories, research, and models of human learning to achieve its intended outcomes.	People learn by doing. Students learn from teachers modeling and then students doing. *The Startup Teacher Playbook* process provides teachers the space to practice what they preach and empowers them to truly *model* 21st century leadership skills and then help students do them, too.
IMPLEMENTATION: Professional learning that increases educator effectiveness and results for all students applies research on change and sustains support for implementation of professional learning for long-term change.	*The Startup Teacher Playbook* process provides space to explore up-to-date, relevant research about any given topic. When implemented as a team, level, or faculty, the process has built-in support as educators build off of and rely on each other for feedback, ideas, and encouragement, fostering long-term change from the ground up.
OUTCOMES: Professional learning that increases educator effectiveness and results for all students aligns its outcomes with educator performance and student curriculum standards.	When educators are empowered to work on issues about which they are passionate, performance (engagement, energy) improves. When students are involved in crafting curriculum that is meaningful to them (while meeting standards), they are more engaged and excited about learning. *The Startup Teacher Playbook* process emphasizes both of these as part of the problem-solving and project management process.

Get Credit

As you work your way through the Canvas and implement your ideas, use the following Impact Log* (*available to download at theeducatorslab.com*) to track hours and reflect on your work.** If you plan to host a workshop for educators, a great way to get buy-in is to make sure participants get credit for their work. Use the Impact Log in conjunction with any of the workshop and brainstorming ideas in this section to build your own PD experience.

Sample Credit/Recertification Requirements

Directions:

1. Attend _____ Workshop/Brainstorming session(s). (_____ hours)

2. Complete the Educator Canvas to provide an overview of your project. (_____ hours)

3. Complete the Impact Log documenting the hours and tasks you complete to implement your project.

4. Provide supporting evidence to showcase your work (*e.g., before and after photos, video, surveys from students, student work, etc.*).

5. Project must be _____ hours of activity. It does not need to be consecutive.

Completed Canvas Due_____ Completed Impact Log Due _____
Submit to _____ at _____
Contact _____ at _____ for questions and/or additional support.

Grading Requirements

Participants are expected to:

- Actively participate in a brainstorming workshop;

- Complete and submit their Educator Canvas (for feedback);

- Implement their idea(s), documenting their process using the Impact Log.

Successful projects will be evaluated on the following:

1. Effort. It's okay if your solution is not successful, but you will need to reflect on what you've learned.

2. Detailed completion of the Educator Canvas (may be done in a different format; simply include all the same information).

3. Detailed Impact Log (may be done in a different format; simply include all the same information).

4. Clear supporting evidence (will vary depending on project), such as before/after photos, videos, student work, and surveys that demonstrate implementation and support your documentation.

*Inspired by Kari Wardle, Idaho PBS
**Credit and recertification requirements vary by state. Use and adapt the following form to fit the standards of your state or local accrediting agency.

Impact Log

Additional Preparation/Planning

You've completed the Educator Canvas but might need to take a few more steps before you can start implementation. Example: You may need to gather user input, research a few apps, or read an article or two. Document any time you spend and activities you do to prep for your project. Then add notes connecting the task to your end goal (explain the WHY).

Actions Taken:

Dates/ Hours	Description of Tasks	Connection: *Why* this matters or is helpful

Implementation

List the core steps and activities you did to implement your project. It's okay if the tasks and to-dos have evolved since you completed the Canvas. Remember, it's an organic process. Then reflect on how it went, the impact it had (or didn't have), what you learned, and what you might change if you did this project again.

Dates/ Hours	Description of Process	Reflection

Evaluation

Did your solution address your challenge? Why or why not? How did it impact your user? Your teaching? Your feelings about teaching? Your day-to-day approach or process in the classroom? Be specific and provide examples when possible.

Analysis of Impact

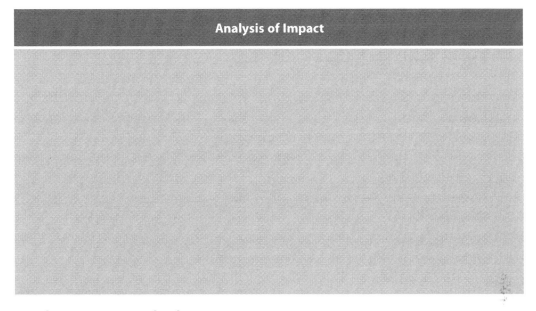

Final Summary and Observations

What did you take away from this process? Anything you learned or important adjustments you had to make throughout the implementation phase? What would you do differently if you could do this project again? What's next for you (e.g., do you plan to take this project to the next level or try something else)?

Wrap-up and Reflection

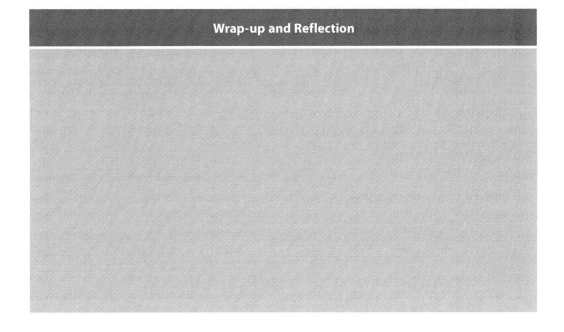

Facilitating Your Own PD: Brainstorming Ideas

Great conversations are so valuable. We use them to build relationships as they encourage us to ask, listen, and understand others' viewpoints. We're better able to understand our challenges and implement solutions when we uncover others' needs.

Here are a few of our favorite ways to generate conversations via brainstorming activities. Get talking and get ready to go deep and learn from others.

Conversation Menu

This tool is perfect for small-group discussion. We love it because it can generate *a lot* of ideas in a short amount of time.

Directions:

Use this template to engage others in a deep conversation about a topic of choice.

Step 1: Create a theme for your conversation menu.

Step 2: Pick a starter question that engages them in the topic and preps them for the "main course."

Step 3: Pick three varying questions that allow participants to get into the "meat" of what you want them to discuss.

Step 4: Pick two possible questions to help participants synthesize their conversation and wrap up their ideas.

Topic:

STARTER

Discuss the question   10 min

MAIN COURSE

Pick one of the three questions   20 min

DESSERT

Pick one of the two questions   20 min

Gum Ball Discussion

Give participants (students, colleagues) three to five sheets of different-colored paper. For each color, assign a different concept or topic (see examples). Everyone completes each color "task," crumples up each piece of paper to make "gum balls," and then tosses them around the room. Once the gum ball machine is thoroughly mixed, everyone gathers one page of each color. Begin your activity.

EXAMPLES:

English class: Red = type of conflict; Yellow = a location; Green = an inciting incident; Blue = two lines of dialogue; Orange = one to three generic characters. Once you have your papers, write a story using those elements.

Math class: Each color of paper represents a different type of math problem. Students write a sample problem of each "color." Once they have new papers, solve the problems.

At a meeting: Give each color a topic or focus. Have staff/colleagues write their thoughts about that topic. Toss around the papers like gum balls. Where you go next is up to you!

Topic Ideas for Staff Meetings:

- If you could wave a magic wand and fix one thing at this school, what would you do?

- List two goals you think we should have for the upcoming year (for students/staff/district).

- What is your biggest pet peeve about working here right now?

- What ideas have you heard about (from reading, other schools, Twitter, etc.) that you'd like to explore?

- What are the kids (parents/guardians, community members) complaining about?

- At my dream school, I would _____.

- In my ideal classroom, students would _____.

Then discuss and brainstorm as you like!

Fishbowl

We love fishbowls because they offer a great window into people's perspectives, opinions, and feelings. It's best to run these with a medium-sized group (we find twenty to thirty people an ideal size).

Step 1: Pick a Topic. Use a question or statement. The more open-ended, the more conversation you will have.

Step 2: Set the Scene. The more informal it feels, the better. Have half of your participants sit in a circle in the middle, facing each other, and the other half sit in an exterior circle on the outside, where they can observe the dialogue.

Step 3: Timing and Structure. Decide how much time to allot, and how you want to run the fishbowl.

- Give participants time to reflect on the topic and collect their thoughts.

- Decide how much time to devote toward actual discussion. Common methods:

  ▸ Have a Group A and Group B, and switch midway into discussion time.

  ▸ Have participants tap other participants to switch in and out.

- Allot a bit of time to debrief and wrap up the conversation.

Step 4: Get Started. Go over the rules and norms of the fishbowl so participants know what to expect, then share the topic and get going!

Starbursting (Adapted from Source Tutorial)

The 5Ws and How are famous for a reason. Use them to generate questions about your problem or solution so you can dig deeper.

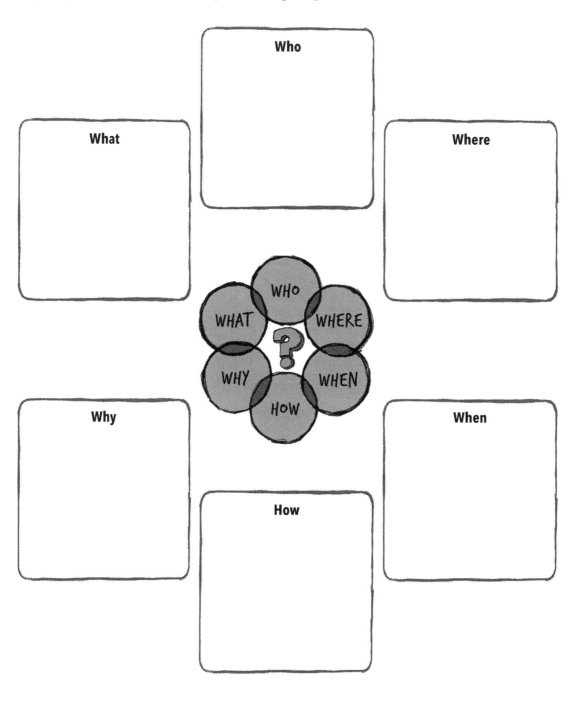

What If ...

An easy game, but not always obvious. Ask everyone in the room to finish the question with the first answer that comes to mind. Push their thinking by offering crazy what ifs (e.g., What if you had $10 million to fix this problem? What if your grandma was in charge of fixing this?).

What if...

What if...

Conversation Facilitation Tips

No matter what brainstorming or workshop activity you try, your goal should be to motivate teachers to *action*. Any of the conversation starters included here could be an opening activity for a TeacherHack or session using the Educator Canvas. No matter what, make sure taking action is the end result and focus of this activity. Yes, venting is helpful, but empower teachers to create, fix, and change.

Ideas to Allow Conversation and Start Organizing

- Break into groups. Give each group one color of "gum balls" or one "menu" to discuss. Then instruct them to write the top one to three ideas (can be partially based on repeated suggestions, partially from group discussion) onto big sheets of paper to share out.

- Collect all brainstorming materials. As a large group (or using a group of volunteers), organize the comments, focusing on common themes.

- Give each person a random brainstorming sheet to read. Have them rank what they think are the top two ideas/suggestions/pressing issues. Then think-pair-share and grow a list of common themes.

Ideas to Share the Findings; Narrow Down the Choices

- Post topics around the room. Do a gallery walk so everyone can read the most common issues that came up.

- Create a survey listing the top topics (either overall or from each category). Have staff rank the ideas.

- Do a staff think-pair-share. Share top gum balls, then re-rank as a team of two. Teams of two then think-pair-share with another team of two, re-ranking again based on what's shared. You can do another round or have those teams of four share with the whole group.

Ideas to Make a Choice

- Give each staff member two to four stickers. Have them vote by placing a sticker on the issues they feel most need to be addressed. They can cast all their votes on one topic or divide them up as they wish.

- Send out a survey.

- Take a vote.

- Divide into level teams (or any other meaningful preexisting groups) and allow each team to pick a topic about which they feel most passionate.

- Have them stand by the topic they most want to address (no matter how hard they think it will be).

Ideas to Take Action

You will likely need a general plan for this step before you even begin. Consider:

- When: Can you use monthly staff meetings for this work? Level/team meetings? Volunteer time? Provide credit for those interested?

- Who: Allow teachers to choose their topic to increase buy-in.

- How far can they go: Do not allow teachers to work on coming up with a solution if the district is not prepared to follow their recommendations!

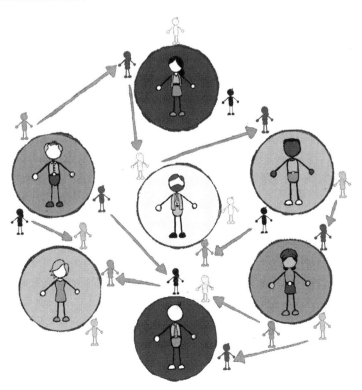

Facilitating Your Own PD: The Educator Canvas Workshop

Whether as a stand-alone workshop or an add-on to any sit-and-get PD, the Educator Canvas enables educators to play with, tinker, and explore new ideas. Provide time for follow-through and implementation. Print out the Canvas and run a workshop yourself. Use tips from the book to lead others through the process, tap into the brainstorming activities, or find a format that works best for *you*.

Think about:

Step 1: Establish your goals.	• Do you want participants to work as individuals or teams? • Do you want them to work on their own ideas or develop a solution to a challenge you've already selected? • Will participants get credit for doing this work (e.g., recertification hours)?
Step 2: Decide on the format.	• Will participants need time to devote to hashing out their problems or for brainstorming their solutions? This might require additional activities or support. • Will this process be done over half a day, a day, or over the course of the year? In an ideal world, you might have a day to focus on the challenge, a day to focus on brainstorming solutions, a day to focus on the Canvas, a support day, and a wrap-up day. Get creative. Larger projects require more time and support. • Do you want to make this an add-on to an existing workshop or meeting, so people have the opportunity to think through the implementation of new ideas? • What supplemental activities might you include to make this event more successful and engaging for your audience?
Step 3: Provide support.	• How can you act as a coach or mentor throughout this process? • What support structures might you put in place (e.g., office hours, check-ins)? • Do you need additional resources to run your workshop?
Step 4: Determine follow-through.	• How will you ensure implementation of ideas? • How might you celebrate successes?

Note: Participants may need additional time and support to investigate their challenges and decide on the problems they want to address. They might also need a space to brainstorm their solutions. We've provided a variety of tips and strategies to help you facilitate those dialogues here in Module Five, as well as in Module Two.

Note: Want to give PD credit for this work? Requirements vary by state, so see if you can use our form and adapt it to fit the standards of your local agency.

Overcoming Obstacles: Tips for Conquering Common Roadblocks

Tips, ideas, and strategies for navigating through the basic yet trickier areas that prevent innovation and problem-solving.

Nothing in this section is new; you likely know all of this. But sometimes hearing it again makes it stick.

Time

A universal woe in education: When am I going to do that? Here are a few ideas and reminders on how to "create" more time for collaboration and problem-solving.

1. Get Organized.

- Buy a planner, use your favorite app—whatever helps you keep track of deadlines, important events, and activities—so you know when you need to get things done.

- Make a place for everything. Nothing is worse than wasting time on searching. Create a space for everything so you always know where to look.

- Build a class routine. Use a consistent medium for students to turn in assignments, communicate with parents, etc., to keep your classroom running smoothly.

- Create a one-stop resource shop. Everything's virtual now. How do you organize all the documents/tools? Figure out how you want to organize your tech (Google Drive, Cloud, Slack, Wakelet).

- Tap into support. Think parents, volunteers, and teaching assistants. Give clear roles, expectations, and tasks so they can make your life easier.

- Have backup resources for emergencies. Create a few generic lesson plans for those random sick days, a new student packet for unexpected additions, and common forms readily available for stressful days when you might need them.

I'd like to try ...

I'd like help with ...

I'll reach out to ...

My emergency preparedness kit needs to include ...

2. Ditch Time-Wasters.

Personal

- Are you on social media more than you'd like (e.g., your phone alerts you that you average three hours or more of screen time each day)?
- Can you get rid of unnecessary distractors (e.g., too much TV)?

School

- Have a specific time when you check email, and stick to it.
- Respect your alone time (don't feel bad if you have to close your door or politely say you need to work).
- Avoid gossip, which kills time and energy.

3. Rethink How You Use Meeting Time and Space.

- Can you cancel or skip unnecessary meetings?
- Can you provide more structure to mandatory meetings or planning time so they don't feel like a time-suck?

4. Model How to Share Information Efficiently.

- Utilize emails and attachments as much as you can. Try Voxer for quick, important messages that are catered to a specific individual.

- Research says people retain more information from reading PowerPoint slides themselves than having them read to them. It may feel like you're not doing anything, but there's nothing wrong with sending PowerPoints via email or Drive and telling people to read them.

- Create a parent newsletter or website. Keep them in the know and you will prevent unnecessary emails and redundancy.

Reflect on how you can maximize your *time*.

I'd like to …

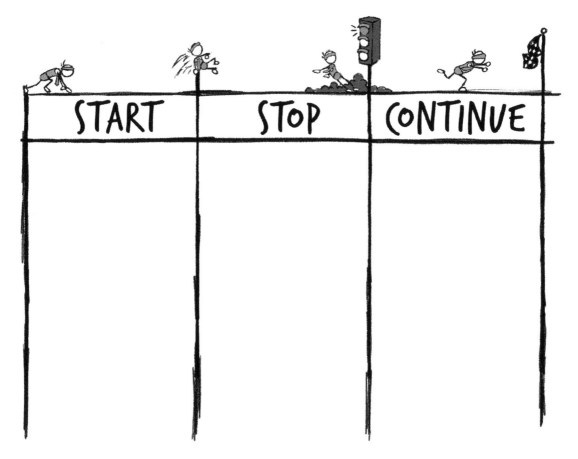

Space

Where can collaboration and problem-solving take place? This section overlaps a bit with time, but here we'll focus less on making time and more on rethinking how we structure the time we do have and reimagining the spaces we use.

1. The Faculty Lounge

Is it a place for the Xerox machine or is it a space that sparks conversation and collaboration?

- Can you turn this into a makerspace?

- Can you create two faculty lounges—one as a quiet workspace and another as a dynamic space for collaboration?

2. The Library

Is it just for the kids, or is it a place to tinker and play with new ideas?

3. The Faculty Meeting

This is often the space where everyone gathers to stay up-to-date and informed. Picture what this looks like at your school. Is it interactive or is it top-down? Here are our favorite ideas:

The Micro Faculty Meeting. Monthly meetings held over the course of two days where leadership meets with smaller groups of teachers throughout the school day in lieu of one big meeting. This style is great when you're working on a collaborative initiative, want to ensure that teachers are driving the decision-making, or simply want to ensure that all teachers have a chance to voice their opinions.

The Flipped Faculty Meeting. Leadership sends out the staff meeting agenda (e.g., PowerPoint) in advance so that staff can review and spend meeting time working together. This format is great when you need a practical way to disseminate information, but still allow for input.

The Edcamp-style Faculty Meeting. Faculty meeting time is broken up into breakout sessions selected and led by colleagues. It's ideal when you want staff to have the opportunity to learn from one another.

Reimagine how you can use *space*.

I'd like to ...

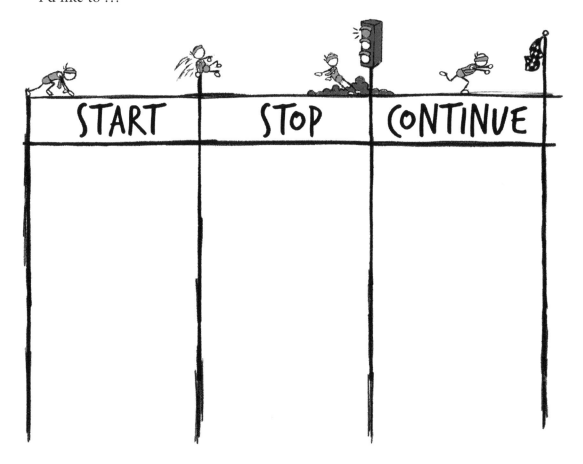

Money

Yup, everything has a price. Here are ideas that we've found to be successful on how to get the funds you need to make change happen for our classrooms.

1. Crowdfunding

A process of raising money in small amounts from a large number of donors. Great for small projects. Many crowdfunding options are out there, with options for how to tell your story and get the most engagement. Here are our favorites:

DonorsChoose continues to be the leader in helping teachers fund classroom projects. They also offer great advice on getting your project funded.

Adopt-a-Classroom enables you to set up a classroom page so funds go toward your goals/initiatives.

Piggybackr helps students raise their own funds for things like team outings, uniforms, field trips, or other pricey learning experiences. The site caters to young students as well.

2. Sponsors

Often the fastest way to get the funds you need is to find someone who cares about your cause.

For specific asks: Think about who you know, who your students know, and who's in your community. Could a company contribute to your cause? Can you send word out to family members and friends to get their support?

For school supplies: Apply to be a part of organizations that can support your classroom or school. If a certain percent of your students qualify for free/reduced lunch, you may be able to partner with an organization and receive support (although it may not be exactly what you need for your specific project). Think Kids in Need Foundation, but check out other local or national options.

3. Grants and Micro-Grants

Grants have a bad reputation for being time-consuming and expensive, but that's not always the case. For many projects, a micro-grant (meaning a grant for a small sum of money—think $250–$1,000) could suffice for your project. Also, professional learning grants help you take your learning to the next level.

Ideas on where to look:

- Google Edutopia's Big List of Education Grants to see what's out there.

- Sites like grants4teachers provide you with a database of grants, as well as grant-writing tips.

Tips:

- Follow the directions closely. Give them only what they ask for.

- Make sure your project fits into their objectives.

4. Beyond Money: Resources, Freebies

Do you actually need money? Maybe a company or individual can offer you the resources you need, instead. Is there a more cost-effective way to get what you need? So many ways exist to get resources and people to help you out. Perhaps you need to get creative.

- Drive around on Saturday morning and hit up yard sales.

- See if a parent will help you build what you need out of the supplies you have.

- Check out online sites where people are giving stuff away. You may have to arrange pick-up, but people may be giving away what you need (and for free).

- Talk to your administration.

- Talk to your PTA.

- Talk to your custodian: they know where to find things.

- **Ask!** Put a request in your school newsletter or Facebook/Twitter feed; contact your local paper and see if they will post a request; seek out community notice boards; contact your local Chamber of Commerce.

Reflect on how you might find the money/resources/supplies for your work.

Data

Data is the love/hate game for most of us in the innovation space. If you need buy-in from other stakeholders (e.g., parents or admin), it's good to have a credible source that lays a foundation for why your project is worth pursuing. The more novel your idea, the less data you may have to back it up, but you can often back up your rationale.

1. Proof of Concept

It's hard to innovate in the education space because people often want data to back up your idea before you can pilot it. Well, you can't get data unless you try, thus the catch-22 that is data/innovation in education. View your idea as a hypothesis and look for data that can show a proof of concept that verifies your point.

2. Brand

We're a bit sad to say this, but from our experience, it's not always about how good the idea is, but rather who backs it up.

- Is there a university professor who might vouch for this? (FYI, reaching out to university faculty is easier than you may think. Use what you learned from pitching.)

- An author?

- Have you tried blogging about this idea and getting published in a well-known source? Try to find a way to get an official stamp on your work or ideas so people take it more seriously.

The Data Game: A Love/Hate Relationship

We say "data game" because we constantly hear about the desire for innovation in education, yet people want data to prove a concept works. How do you prove it works before you've had a chance to try it? How do you find the time to gather this data? Back up your problem's importance when you don't have much data available about your solution.

The love/hate stems from some data being beyond helpful (big studies that show immense student gains thanks to a targeted practice) and some data that sucks and doesn't tell us what we need to know. Test scores can give a snapshot, but don't tell the story of a student.

When considering data, trust your gut. Does this data help students? Could this data help support your argument?

Printables

Here are our collaborative problem-solving tools in one easy spot. Our goal was to create tools to help us use that precious time as efficiently and effectively as possible. We hope that by providing structure we can help teachers make the magic happen. You can also download these tools for free at theeducatorslab.com.

The Needs Tool

This tool enables teachers to reflect on their practice, think through goals, and prioritize challenges. It enables them to develop a single challenge question so they create a common language and vision around the issue they wish to address.

Use this tool as a team or as an individual to:

- Prioritize ideas and identify a problem to tackle.
- Establish personal and/or team buy-in to work collaboratively on something.

The Investigation Tool

This tool challenges individuals and teams to dig deeper into an identified challenge. It encourages them to look at the problem from different lenses so they can develop the most effective solution possible. Use this tool as a team or as an individual to:

- Uncover the key factors that will make or break your project.
- Identify opportunities and constraints.

The Brainstorming Tool

This tool encourages teachers and teams to expand their thinking around how they could address a challenge. It emphasizes the need to stay on task with goals and to consider the needs of the learner. Use this tool as a team or as an individual to:

- Develop solutions that emphasize the needs and values of those you're designing for.

The Educator Canvas

This is a project management tool that helps teachers or teams think through all aspects of implementation. It helps teachers create a viable action plan and accountability for their project. Use this tool as a team or as an individual to:

- Develop a concrete strategy to get ideas off the ground.
- Establish project goals and ensure follow-through.

The Needs Tool

Getting Started
What do I work on?

What are your most pressing frustrations? (Think big and small)	What are your main goals for this school year? For the next five years?	What's been on your "to-do" list to improve or to try?	What might students, colleagues, or parents say are problem areas?

Funnel Your Ideas

Pick your top THREE areas that ultimately seem to have the most impact on your students.

1)

2)

3)

PICK THE ONE THAT IS MOST NECESSARY AND PRACTICAL.

Frame what you want to work on as a question:

How might I/we ___ACTION___ + ___USER___ + ___IMPACT___ ?

CHALLENGE QUESTION

The Investigation Tool

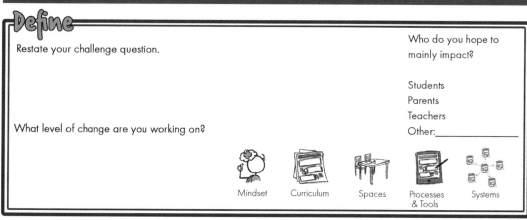

Investigate Your Challenge

What do you need to KNOW to design the BEST possible response to your challenge?

Define

Restate your challenge question.

What level of change are you working on?

Who do you hope to mainly impact?

Students
Parents
Teachers
Other:_____

Mindset   Curriculum   Spaces   Processes & Tools   Systems

CONSIDER!

Check out blogs, social media, podcasts, or articles to see how others are tackling this issue. List at least FIVE of your favorite pieces of inspiration.

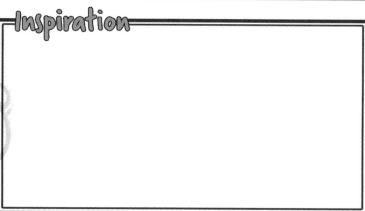

Inspiration

Observations

CONSIDER!

Write down everything you've noticed about your challenge.

Investigate Your Challenge (Continued)

CONSIDER!

Share your challenge with students and colleagues. Note their observations and opinions on the matter.

Input

Experience

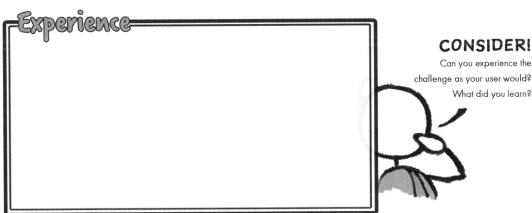

CONSIDER!

Can you experience the challenge as your user would? What did you learn?

Discoveries

List your top three takeaways from your investigation.

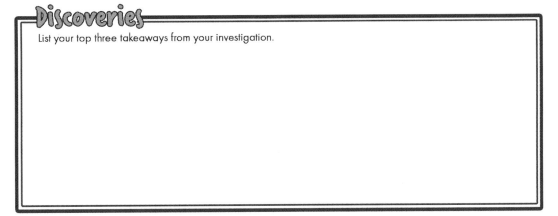

The Brainstorming Tool

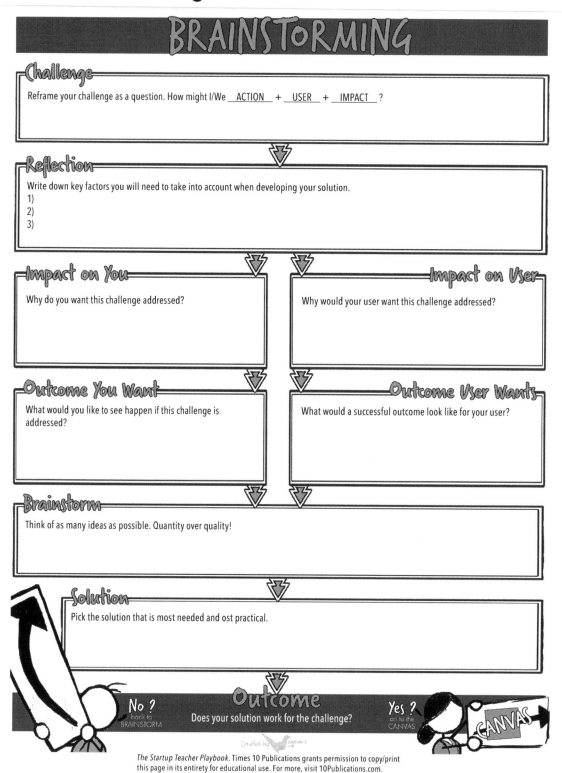

BRAINSTORMING

Challenge
Reframe your challenge as a question. How might I/We __ACTION__ + __USER__ + __IMPACT__ ?

Reflection
Write down key factors you will need to take into account when developing your solution.
1)
2)
3)

Impact on You
Why do you want this challenge addressed?

Impact on User
Why would your user want this challenge addressed?

Outcome You Want
What would you like to see happen if this challenge is addressed?

Outcome User Wants
What would a successful outcome look like for your user?

Brainstorm
Think of as many ideas as possible. Quantity over quality!

Solution
Pick the solution that is most needed and ost practical.

Outcome
No ?
back to
BRAINSTORM

Does your solution work for the challenge?

Yes ?
on to the
CANVAS

CANVAS

Created by

The Educator Canvas

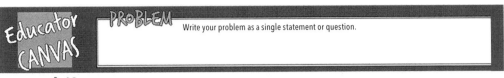

Educator CANVAS

PROBLEM Write your problem as a single statement or question.

Project Name

Short-Term Goals

What would success look like?
How might you measure your goals?
How is your project creating value for others?

Inspiration

What evidence can you find to validate that this idea could work?
What tools or strategies could you use or adapt to help you implement?

Long-Term Vision

Is this a one-off project or a piece of a bigger picture?
How do short-term goals fit into a longer-term vision?

User Input

How will you get buy-in from your user?
How do you plan to get feedback on your solution from your user?

IMPACT

INSIGHTS

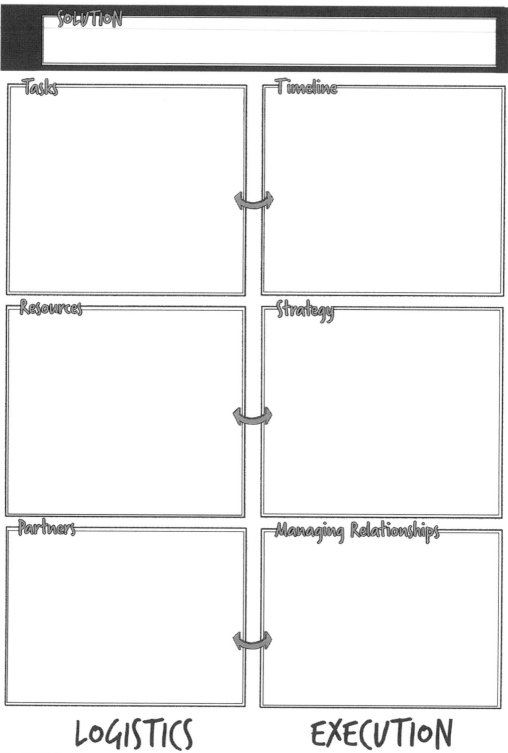

SOLUTION

Tasks

Timeline

Resources

Strategy

Partners

Managing Relationships

LOGISTICS

EXECUTION

About the Authors

Michelle Blanchet

Michelle is an educational consultant striving to improve how we treat, train, and value our teachers. After ten years of experience working with young people, she founded the Educators' Lab, which supports teacher-driven solutions to educational challenges. Michelle earned a Master's in International Relations from Instituto de Empresa in Madrid. She has taught social studies in Switzerland and the U.S. and has presented at numerous events, including SXSWedu and TEDxLausanne. Michelle is a part of the Global Shaper Community of the World Economic Forum. She has worked with organizations like PBS Education, the Center for Transformative Teaching and Learning, Ashoka, and the Center for Curriculum Redesign. Originally from Virginia, she now resides in Switzerland with her husband and three daughters. You can find her online at www.theeducatorslab.com or @Educatorslab.

Darcy Bakkegard

Darcy is a veteran classroom teacher who became a professional development and technology integration coach to create PD that empowers teachers to implement their ideas to improve teaching and learning. Darcy has a Master's of Secondary Education in English, is an ISTE Certified Educator, and has conducted countless workshops and presentations locally, nationally, and internationally. After teaching English and theatre in public and private, rural and suburban, and international schools, she now serves as a freelance professional development coach and trainer specializing in interactive strategies for the classroom, meaningful technology integration, and teacher-driven problem-solving workshops. Darcy lives in Fargo, North Dakota, with her husband, Jeff, and triplets Kurtis, Benjamin, and Cordelia. Find her online at darcy@theeducatorslab.io or @dbakkegard on Twitter.

Acknowledgments

To our mothers: Thank you for the countless hours of care you've provided for our little ones (and for us). Thank you for your perspective as educators. This book wouldn't exist without you.

To our fathers: Thank you for your positive encouragement and coaching. Your endless belief in us is a gift everyone should receive.

To our husbands: Thank you for serving as our harshest critics and constant support systems. You made this book better (and kept the kids alive).

To the Times 10 team: Thank you for your insights, patience, and flexibility as you helped make this dream of ours a reality.

To the teachers—those we've worked alongside, those we've coached, and those we've turned to for advice: Thank you for doing this work. You are our inspiration and we hope this book can help support you and your students.

Thank you!

More from
TIMES 10

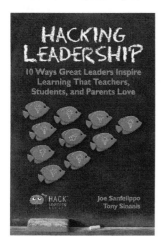

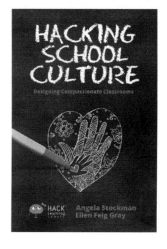

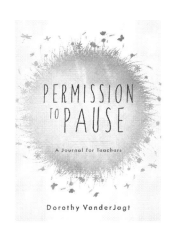

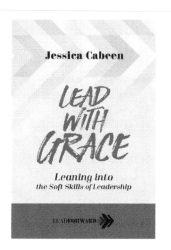

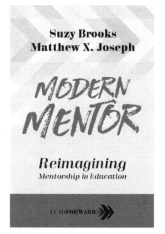

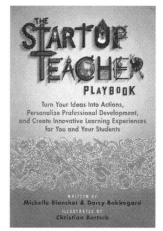

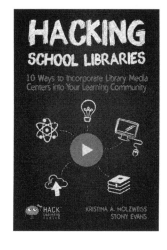

Resources from Times 10

10Publications.com

**Join the Times 10 Ambassadors
and help us revolutionize education:**
10Publications.com/ambassador

Podcasts:
hacklearningpodcast.com
jamesalansturtevant.com/podcast

On Twitter:
@10Publications
@HackMyLearning
#Times10News
@LeadForward2
#LeadForward
#HackLearning
#HackingLeadership
#MakeWriting
#HackingQs
#HackingSchoolDiscipline
#LeadWithGrace
#QuietKidsCount
#ModernMentor
#AnxiousBook

All things Times 10:
10Publications.com

Vision, Experience, Action
10PUBLICATIONS.COM

TIMES 10 provides practical solutions that busy educators can read today and use tomorrow. We bring you content from experts, shared through books, podcasts, and an array of social networks. Our books bring Vision, Experience, and Action to educators around the world. Stay in touch with us at 10Publications.com and follow our updates on Twitter @10Publications and #Times10News.

Made in the USA
Columbia, SC
02 February 2021